Conquering
INSECURITY

Deborah
Smith Pegues

HARVEST HOUSE PUBLISHERS

EUGENE, OREGON

Cover by Koechel Peterson & Associates, Inc., Minneapolis, Minnesota

CONQUERING INSECURITY
Copyright © 2005 by Deborah Smith Pegues
Published by Harvest House Publishers
Eugene, Oregon 97402

Library of Congress Cataloging-in-Publication Data

Pegues, Deborah Smith, 1950–
  Conquering insecurity / Deborah Smith Pegues.
    p. cm.
  ISBN–13: 978-0-7369-1569-4 (pbk.)
  ISBN–10: 0-7369-1569-9 (pbk.)
  1. Self-confidence—Religious aspects—Christianity. 2. Security (Psychology) I. Title.
  BV4598.23.P44   2005
  248.4—dc22   2005001909

Printed in the United States of America

06 07 08 09 10 11 12 / VP-CF / 10 9 8 7 6 5 4 3

*This book is dedicated to my husband, Darnell,
my companion, my confidant, and my cheerleader.
There is none like you on all the earth.*

Acknowledgments

Special thanks...

To the Harvest House family: Bob Hawkins Jr., president, for his humility, his passion, and his commitment to the spiritual development of those who love to read; Terry Glaspey, director of acquisitions and development, who stretched me beyond my comfort zone to do a thorough work; Kim Moore, my editor, who convinced me that I could do it; and the entire staff for the spirit of team that makes the company the powerhouse that it is.

To P.B. "Bunny" Wilson, for her wisdom and godly example of what an emotionally secure woman really looks like.

To my friends in ministry: Terri McFadden, Theresa McFadden, Sandra Arceneaux, Marilyn Beaubien, and Pat Ashley, for their encouragement.

To my Bible study group: LaTanya Richardson Jackson, Cookie Johnson, Charlayne Woodard, Akousua Busia, Wanda Vaughn, Andi Chapman, Candida Mobley-Wright, Eula Smith, Jennifer McHenry, Cheri Townsend, Patricia Moore, and Pat Kelly, whose hunger and receptivity for the Word kept me researching the principles discussed herein.

To everyone who participated anonymously so that the world could benefit from your story.

To my family, for your unwavering support of all I do.

To my husband, Darnell, who had to endure my hours of solitude and unavailability in order to bring the book to fruition.

Most of all, to my Lord, who is indeed the author and finisher of this work.

Contents

The Root of Insecurity 7

PART I
SEVEN SYNDROMES
OF INSECURITY

Syndrome 1: The Saul Syndrome 15
Justifying Jealousy

Syndrome 2: The Eliab Syndrome 21
Exhibiting Envy

Syndrome 3: The Haman Syndrome 31
Seeking Significance

Syndrome 4: The Diotrephes Syndrome 37
Preserving Preeminence

Syndrome 5: The Aaron Syndrome 47
Pleasing People

Syndrome 6: The Ahithophel Syndrome 53
Performing or Perishing

Syndrome 7: The Elihu Syndrome 63
Imagining Inadequacy

PART II
SEVEN ROADBLOCKS
TO SUPREME CONFIDENCE

Roadblock 1: Prayerlessness 71

Roadblock 2: Personal Devaluation 81

Roadblock 3: Poor Knowledge 87

Roadblock 4: Purposeless Living 95

Roadblock 5: Past Transgressions 101

Roadblock 6: Perfectionism 107

Roadblock 7: Pride 119

PART III
SEVEN STRATEGIES FOR CONQUERING THE GIANT OF INSECURITY

Strategy 1: Rest on God's Word...................... 129

Strategy 2: Refuse to Be Deterred.................... 133

Strategy 3: Remember Past Victories.................. 137

Strategy 4: Reject Carnal Weapons................... 141

Strategy 5: Resist Intimidation...................... 147

Strategy 6: Run Toward the Giant.................... 151

Strategy 7: Reap the Reward........................ 157

PART IV
SEVEN HABITS OF EMOTIONALLY SECURE PEOPLE

Habit 1: Embracing Individuality 163

Habit 2: Employing Teamwork 169

Habit 3: Engaging Constructive Feedback.............. 179

Habit 4: Establishing Boundaries 187

Habit 5: Empowering Others 199

Habit 6: Enjoying Success 207

Habit 7: Experiencing Peace........................ 217

Walking in Victory................................. 225

Appendix A: Healing Prayer for Insecurity.............. 227

Appendix B: Insecurity-Banishing Scriptures............ 229

Notes.. 233

The Root of Insecurity

HE SUNDAY MORNING WORSHIP SERVICE was in full swing at Faith Covenant Church. Sherry glanced up from her hymnal just in time to see the usher direct a shapely young woman to the seat on the other side of her husband, John. Sherry cringed as she took in the beauty of the sexy latecomer, who looked as if someone had poured her into her way-too-short-for-church spandex dress. Sherry silently scolded herself for abandoning her latest diet program. Of course, John was a loving husband who had never been unfaithful, and he was not prone to wandering eyes. Notwithstanding, Sherry thought of asking him to exchange seats with her, but she decided her motive would have been too obvious.

Across the aisle Jerry, the church plant manager, peeked into the weekly bulletin. What he saw caused him to turn green with envy. Lois Smith, the latest new hire to the church staff, was featured as "Staff Person of the Month." Until the arrival of this highly credentialed superstar, Jerry was the most esteemed member of the staff. Though he had only a high school education, he was one of the founding members of the church. He was faithful in his attendance to scheduled services, and he was the official go-to person for the majority of problems that arose—at least, he was before the church started to experience mega growth. Now the pastor was hiring seasoned professionals with fancy technical and managerial skills. He was even raising his expectations of all paid and volunteer leaders. To Jerry, it seemed his status was eroding by the day.

Finally, in the pulpit Pastor Terry was fretting over the increasing popularity of Elder Moore, the men's Bible study teacher. Why, the attendance in his class was large enough to start a small church! Elder Moore was a great communicator, his messages were relevant, and he was genuinely concerned about the men and their issues. It was no secret that they admired him and considered him their mentor. To boot, he was also a solid and well-balanced family man. Pastor Terry had never heard anyone cast an aspersion on Elder Moore's character. In sum, the guy was virtually perfect. Pastor Terry was torn between viewing him as a valuable asset or a potential liability.

> *Insecurity is an unbelieving mind-set, rooted in fear and nourished by spiritual and natural ignorance.*

What do Sherry, Jerry, and Pastor Terry have in common? They are all battling an unrelenting emotional giant. It is a giant that lives in the mind and causes its victims to feel inadequate, unsure, or doubtful of their abilities to perform in the essential aspects of life. It is the giant of insecurity.

No respecter of persons, insecurity can infiltrate and influence every aspect of a person's life. It attacks individuals from the lowest to the highest rungs of the professional, social, economic, and spiritual ladders. Although it thrives in the mind, insecurity is not a psychological disorder.

Insecurity is an unbelieving mind-set, rooted in fear and nourished by spiritual and natural ignorance. It was my frequent companion until I found out how to recognize and overcome its many manifestations. Even now insecurity sneaks in an occasional visit, but my spiritual radar quickly alerts me to its presence and enables me to respond with appropriate firepower from the Word of God. Notwithstanding, I am not so naive as to believe insecurity will ever stop trying to rear its ugly head in one area or another in my life. That is why I am writing this book.

In the following chapters, I will share the truths that God has revealed to me for conquering this giant. You will be introduced to biblical characters and situations, as well as modern-day people who may mirror your own behavior or that of someone you know. Your relationships will improve as you gain insight into the fears that cause you to behave in certain ways—at home, at work, and at play. You will learn how to stay on high alert for this insidious enemy and how to defeat it each time it rises up in your life.

During the course of our journey, I will also give you instructions on how to leave the valley of self-doubt, bypass the road of self-confidence, and advance to the highway of Supreme confidence.

It is not my intent to provide an in-depth analysis of the numerous circumstances or situations that may have caused a person to become insecure. Suffice to say that insecurity is learned behavior—and it is learned early in life. Its origin may be found in traumatic childhood experiences, such as the loss of a parent through death, divorce, drug abuse, or abandonment; cruel teasing and rejection by other children; rejection by peers during the formative years because of a handicap or other physical "difference"; an overly critical, non-nurturing, non-affirming parent; a prejudiced, unsupportive teacher; an unstable home environment due to numerous job relocations; or financially irresponsible parents, to name a few.

Tracing your various insecurities to their roots would be time well spent. At least you would know the foundation of the problem. Notwithstanding, while it is helpful to understand the path that got you to your current level of insecurity, it is more important to get on the road to recovery. That is what this book is about.

In Part I, Seven Syndromes of Insecurity, we will examine seven biblical characters and look at how their insecurity affected their lives and the lives of others. In Part II, Seven Roadblocks to Supreme Confidence, I will challenge you to take an introspective self-audit of seven behaviors that may be preventing you from becoming the confident person you desire to be. "Supreme confidence," of course, refers to the confidence that only comes from trusting and abiding in the Supreme Being, our heavenly Father. In Part III, Seven Strategies for Conquering the Giant of Insecurity, the battle is on. These chapters parallel the story of David and Goliath and show you how to overcome your insecurities despite obvious realities or discouragement from others.

By the time you reach Part IV, Seven Habits of Emotionally Secure People, you will have conquered the giant—or know how to—and will be poised to model behavior that bespeaks the victory you have achieved through God's grace.

Finally, the appendices feature key information to help you maintain your mastery of insecurity. Appendix A is a powerful, scripturally referenced healing prayer that connects you with God and leads you into declaring your victory on a daily basis. Appendix B is an arsenal of Scriptures for you to memorize, recite, or read each time the giant of insecurity tries to revisit your life.

Quick Self-Assessment

Before you begin your quest for Supreme confidence, let's take a quick assessment of your current level of insecurity. Please answer yes or no to the questions below. Be honest.

Resist the urge to go into denial. Know that an acknowledged weakness can be your greatest strength and the quickest path to an emotionally balanced and fulfilling life.

Insecurity Quiz

1. Do you find yourself resenting or criticizing others who are assertive, confident, or capable in areas in which you feel inadequate?

2. Do you become anxious when it appears that someone may take your place of prominence in a certain environment or relationship?

3. Do you brag about your possessions, accomplishments, or well-known acquaintances in order to gain the admiration of others?

4. Do you become perturbed when someone disagrees with your opinion or rejects your advice?

5. Do you fail to pursue certain opportunities for fear of failure or inadequacy for the task?

6. When working with a team, do you prefer to "shine alone" rather than having the group share the credit for your ideas?

7. Do you resist giving or receiving constructive criticism?

8. Do you find it difficult to say no or to express your personal boundaries or preferences in relationships?

9. Do you feel slighted when someone gives a friend, sibling, coworker, or another person a compliment or an accolade in your presence?

10. Do you feel inadequate or inferior due to certain unchangeable physical features, such as your height, skin color, a physical deformity, a handicap, facial features, or your age?

If you answered yes to any of these questions, you are most likely battling insecurity at some level. If you answered yes to five or more, insecurity has a major hold on your life. Do not despair; conquering it is not impossible. You can break its grip and become an emotionally secure person. Be patient. Understand that this will be a process rather than an event. There is a popular riddle that asks, "How do you eat an elephant?" The answer is, "One bite at a time." And so it is with insecurity. How do you conquer it? One fear at a time. Let's get started.

PART I

SEVEN SYNDROMES
OF INSECURITY

Syn·drome: a distinctive pattern of behavior

The Saul Syndrome

Justifying Jealousy

Anger is cruel, and wrath is like a flood,
but who can survive the
destructiveness of jealousy?

PROVERBS 27:4 NLT

KING SAUL FOUND HIMSELF in a real dilemma. David, an unknown upstart, had killed Goliath, the Philistine giant, and was gaining in popularity daily. In fact, the women were literally singing his praises.

> When the men were returning home after David had killed the Philistine, the women came out from all the towns of Israel to meet King Saul with singing and dancing, with joyful songs and with tambourines and lutes. As they danced, they sang: "Saul has slain his thousands, and David his tens of thousands." Saul was very angry; this refrain galled him. "They have credited David with tens of thousands," he thought, "but me with only thousands. What more can he get but the kingdom?" And from that time on Saul kept a jealous eye on David (1 Samuel 18:6-9).

Angered and humiliated by their song, King Saul embarked upon a campaign to wipe David off the face of the earth. The insecure king was relentless in his pursuit, engaging in repeated attempts to slay the innocent young man whom he now viewed as a rival to his throne (1 Samuel 18–26). David's lifestyle became that of a fugitive as he literally ran from place to place trying to escape the wrath of Saul.

What was this gnawing emotion that fueled Saul's actions? It was raw, unadulterated jealousy—the fear of being displaced. It consumed him like a fire. He was determined not to rest until he eliminated the threat to his kingdom.

We can learn from Saul's example. When we attempt to destroy someone whom we consider to be a threat of any kind—be it professional, relational, or otherwise—we have embarked upon a course that will most assuredly come to a dead end as we reap the results of the negative seeds that are planted. Saul did not succeed in killing David. Rather, he and all of his sons were killed in a battle with the Philistines (1 Samuel 31). David then became king of Israel according to the sovereign plan of God.

The sovereign plan of God is a factor in our lives that we must constantly remind ourselves to consider. When jealousy rears its head and tries to make us fear that we are going to be displaced in any manner or in any circumstances, we need to swat those negative thoughts with Psalm 139:16: "You saw me before I was born. Every day of my life was recorded in your book. Every moment was laid out before a single day had passed" (NLT).

Guarding What's Mine

Like the powerful suction of a vacuum cleaner, jealousy can pull us into its chamber. Once there, we become angry, possessive, fearful, and totally ineffective. There are two truths I try to stay keenly aware of when I sense jealousy's lure. First, God has my back. Second, He has a sovereign plan for my life.

David knew the key to avoiding this trap. He proclaimed, "LORD, you alone are my inheritance, my cup of blessing. You guard all that is mine" (Psalm 16:5 NLT). I have come to understand that when God has determined that something is mine, I have no need to guard it in the sense of watching over it for fear it will escape. That's God's job, not mine. My responsibility is to nurture and enjoy the blessing on a daily basis, rather than obsessing over whether it will still be mine tomorrow. Embracing this truth can free you from anxiety about the unknown. On the other hand, when God, in His wisdom, has decided that something is not to be mine, then I must submit to His plan and release it. Holding on to it will keep me in the pit of insecurity as the thing continues to elude me. Sure, I will need God's supernatural intervention to help me to let it go, but at least I know His empowering grace is available for the asking. I absolutely must trust God to guard what is mine. When a child of God succumbs to the pitfall of jealousy, he engages in the ultimate act of unbelief.

The fear of being displaced knows no economic, social, or political boundaries. Consider Norman McGowan's story:

> It was Sir Winston Churchill's standing order that when he returned by train from a trip that his dog Rufus should be brought to the station to meet him. Rufus would be let off his leash to dash to his master and be the first to greet him. One day I happened to be standing close by. Rufus ignored his master and came leaping all over me instead. Of course, Sir Winston loved Rufus too much to blame him. Instead, he turned to me with a hurt look and said quietly, "In the future, Norman, I would prefer you to stay in the train until I've said hello."[1]

The Jealous Mate

"But," you may be saying, "I'm not the jealous one. How do I deal with my mate's jealousy?" If you are committed to staying in your relationship, you must understand the root cause of your mate's fear of being displaced.

Take the case of a man I will call Kory. He is the illegitimate son of Ronald, a man highly regarded in his community for his wealth and influence. Now, Kory's mother, Wanda, was close friends with Ronald's wife. When Kory was born, Wanda was too embarrassed by her betrayal to disclose the name of Kory's father. However, when Kory reached high school, his mother told him the truth about his birth. By then Ronald's wife had separated from him and moved to another state.

Kory related to me that one day he was downtown shopping with Ronald when they met one of Ronald's friends, who remarked about their striking resemblance. The inquisitive friend went on to ask, "Is this your boy?" Ronald refused to answer directly and deflected the question with a lighthearted reply. Kory was devastated. He took Ronald's response as rejection of him. He wanted his father to be proud to acknowledge him. Kory never told Ronald how that incident had affected him. He chose rather to hide his hurt and to mentally rehearse the incident every chance he got so that he could feel sorry for himself. To this day, Kory has had a challenge with each woman whom he has attempted to relate to romantically. His ex-wife confided to me that during their marriage he was extremely jealous. He even confessed to me that he had often felt that the women in his life would eventually abandon him. Kory allowed one incident to destroy his ability to trust.

Dealing with an Insecure Mate

If you are dealing with an insecure mate, you must make every effort to be accountable. It is important to voluntarily provide adequate (read: *extra*) details to an insecure person. After all, he is looking for assurance. Learn to explain your whereabouts in a casual but thorough manner. Short, one-syllable responses will only provide more insecurity and leave the person to imagine various negative scenarios. After all, the jealous person is insecure and thus feels he does not have what it takes to maintain the relationship.

Do not make the mistake of thinking or saying, "Tough, you just need to get over your insecurity." If it were that easy, he would have done so by now. Continue to pray for his or her healing from this debilitating mind-set, but do your part not to exacerbate the problem with vague communication. Most of all, encourage your partner to talk about his or her fears. Listen without being critical or judgmental. Seek first to understand. Make it clear that you have pure intentions regarding your relationship. But here is something important to keep in mind: Stay balanced in your interaction. You must also make it clear that you will not be forced into an emotional prison by having to account for every moment of the day. This too could exacerbate the jealousy and set up unrealistic expectations. Trust is a two-way street.

Wisdom vs. Insecurity

Some situations may require you to exercise the kind of wisdom that could cause others to accuse you of being insecure. For example, no matter how faithful your husband is, it is probably not a good idea to allow your girlfriend to spend the weekend in your home alone with him while you are away. I know of a woman who regularly allowed her husband to take her best friend home late at night. She was devastated when she later discovered they were having an affair. Wisdom would have dictated that she accompany them—even at the risk of appearing to be insecure.

I once asked the wife of a very popular, internationally known minister if she frequently accompanied her husband to his numerous speaking engagements to various cities and countries. She replied very resolutely, "You have to." Of course, this is not to say that men of the cloth should never travel alone. This was simply one woman's way of being a visible safeguard for her husband.

Now, you may say that if an affair is going to happen, it's going to happen anyway. Just know that a wise woman does not serve her husband to another woman on a silver platter.

CONFIDENCE CHALLENGE

⊘· Describe a relational, professional, social, or other situation in which you fear being displaced.

⊘· Write the Scripture below on a separate piece of paper or a card and meditate on it often.

You saw me before I was born. Every day of my life was recorded in your book. Every moment was laid out before a single day had passed (Psalm 139:16 NLT).

⊘· Remind yourself that no one except you and God can affect His plan for your life.

The Eliab Syndrome

Exhibiting Envy

Wrath is cruel, and anger is outrageous;
but who is able to stand before envy?

PROVERBS 27:4 KJV

HAVE YOU EVER BEEN AROUND SOMEONE who reminded you of what you should be, could be, or desire to be? Did you find yourself resenting or unfairly judging the person because you have not had the faith, courage, discipline, or even opportunity to pursue your own goals? If you answered yes to the latter question, you are being held captive by the monster of envy.

Unlike jealousy, the fear of being displaced, envy is a feeling of ill will toward those who possess the thing you want. It is important to understand this difference. Jealousy says, "I am afraid you are going to take what I have." Envy, on the other hand, says, "I want what you have and I resent you for having it!" Envy is one of the most frequently concealed of all emotions. A person is more likely to admit to an uncontrollable temper, a phobia, or any other negative emotion than to acknowledge that he is envious.

Envy can force you into a cycle of resentment and self-doubt as you start to wonder what it is about you that keeps you from getting what you desire. Your discontentment with your situation becomes the breeding ground for insecurity and its debilitating thoughts: "You don't deserve to have that." "You don't have the beauty, the brains, the body, the personality, the social standing, the contacts, or the *whatever* to even dream of such a thing!" Entertaining such negative thoughts can leave you scorching in the desert of envy and longing for just a drop of the blessings that seem to shower others.

> *Envy can force you into a cycle of resentment and self-doubt as you start to wonder what it is about you that keeps you from getting what you desire.*

You must immediately halt your train of thinking and come to grips with the reality that there will always be somebody within your various circles of interaction who will enjoy an advantage you desire. Don't fall into the trap of believing that somebody's life is perfect just because he has something you wish you had. Life is much more complex than that. Everybody has at least one aspect of his existence he wishes were different. Trust me, there is somebody in your circle who envies you for something you possess. Pray a hedge of protection around your emotions so that envy will not drag you into a pit of insecurity and resentment of others.

Resenting Confidence

After God fired King Saul for his disobedience in offering an unauthorized sacrifice, He dispatched Samuel the prophet to anoint a new king for the nation of Israel. He directed him to the house of a man named Jesse, who had eight sons. The moment Samuel laid eyes on Eliab, the eldest son, it was "king at first sight." He could not hide his enthusiasm at the apparent choice:

> "Surely the LORD's anointed stands here before the LORD." But the LORD said to Samuel, "Do not consider his appearance or his height, for I have rejected him. The LORD does not look at the things man looks at. Man looks at the outward appearance, but the LORD looks at the heart" (1 Samuel 16:6-7).

Eliab's tall and handsome appearance made him seem right for this lofty position. His kingly presence had even persuaded Samuel, an anointed, discerning, and seasoned man of God who literally grew up in church. However, God, being all-knowing, saw something in Eliab's heart that disqualified him for the nation's top job.

Seven of Jesse's sons passed before Samuel for consideration. Of course, no one knew that Samuel was on a secret assignment to anoint a new king. They only knew somebody was being anointed for something special. God rejected them all.

Rejection is guaranteed to produce anger that will most often be directed to the one selected rather than the one who has rejected.

> So he [Samuel] asked Jesse, "Are these all the sons you have?" "There is still the youngest," Jesse answered, "but he is tending the sheep." Samuel said, "Send for him; we will not sit down until he arrives." So he sent and had him brought in. He was ruddy, with a fine appearance and handsome features. Then the LORD said, "Rise and anoint him; he is the one" (1 Samuel 16:11-12).

Imagine the thoughts that must have flooded Eliab's mind at this point. "Well, what's up, Lord? I am the oldest son. I thought it was my birthright to be first in line to receive the place of honor or any other prime benefits!" Eliab had to bear the frustration and humiliation of being rejected in favor of his youngest brother. Rejection is guaranteed to produce anger that will most often be directed to the one *selected* rather than the one who has *rejected*. We often see this when a woman catches her man with another woman. She directs her vengeance to the floozy. An ensuing fight between them is commonplace while the man stands by and watches—sometimes with delight.

Eliab, no doubt, harbored feelings of resentment toward David. Resentment is simply unresolved anger that is "re-sent" to the inside. Unfortunately, once you allow resentment to enter your heart, it acts as a free radical producing an emotional cancer. It will eventually manifest itself in some destructive way, whether it is in the form of overeating, shopping excessively, lashing out, being sarcastic, or physically harming others.

> *When an insecure person meets someone who is confident, he will often accuse him of being arrogant or cocky.*

Eliab's envy and resentment came to the forefront while Israel was at war with the Philistines. Jesse sent David to the scene of the battle to take food and other necessities to his brothers who were in King Saul's army. David became righteously indignant when he arrived and heard Goliath, the Philistine giant, taunting and intimidating the Israelites.

> Then David spoke to the men who stood by him, saying, "What shall be done for the man who kills this Philistine and takes away the reproach from Israel? For who is this uncircumcised Philistine, that he should defy the armies of the living God?" And the people

answered him in this manner, saying, "So shall it be done for the man who kills him." Now Eliab his oldest brother heard when he spoke to the men; and Eliab's anger was aroused against David, and he said, "Why did you come down here? And with whom have you left those few sheep in the wilderness? I know your pride and the insolence of your heart, for you have come down to see the battle." And David said, "What have I done now? Is there not a cause?" (1 Samuel 17:26-29 NKJV).

Have you ever noticed that when an insecure person meets someone who is confident, he will often accuse him of being arrogant or cocky? Of all the men present, why was Eliab the only one who reacted so vehemently to David's statements? David had not engaged in behavior that would incite the envy of others, nor did he attempt to embarrass Eliab in any way. In fact, David's questions were not even directed to his brother. Thus, any embarrassment Eliab felt was self-imposed.

As we dig a little deeper into the Scriptures, we can understand the root of his problem. Eliab was tall and physically strong. And though he looked prepared to fight the giant, he ran from him just as everyone else had done. Eliab felt the pressure of his younger brother demonstrating the confidence and courage that had eluded him. To make matters worse, his name meant "God (El) is my father (ab)." As I meditated on this story, the thought came to my mind, "He is wearing the name, but letting Satan run his game!"

Now, before we pass judgment on Eliab, let's look in the mirror. How many of us are wearing the name "Child of God," but letting Satan run his game by allowing the giant of insecurity to control our lives?

Contrary to Eliab's accusation, David was not cocky, he was just convinced—convinced that God would honor His covenant with the Israelites to protect them and to subdue their enemies. Eliab envied David's confidence. And, in the typical fashion of an insecure person, he attempted to devalue the person he envied—even a blood relative.

Family Envy

Perhaps you are part of a family where, by default, you are the CFO (chief family officer) and therefore the designated problem solver. That's my role. And, like me, you've probably had the experience of other family members resenting your ability to take charge of a situation. The truth of the matter is that they envy your confidence in facing issues head-on and your ability to think clearly, soberly, and objectively in resolving them.

A few years ago, an elderly uncle passed away and left his modest estate to my ailing mother, who was his executor. His will stipulated that I was to be the executor in the event that my mother became unable to perform the requisite duties. Indeed, when he passed away, she was emotionally incapable of handling all of the tasks involved in closing an estate. Oh, the family drama that followed. I have never experienced such alienation from relatives with whom I had always enjoyed wonderful relationships. Discussions about me abounded at various family gatherings. "Why does she get to exercise so much authority?" "Who left her in charge?" "She thinks she's smarter than everybody else!" Why, I even had to wage a legal battle with an unscrupulous relative who contested the will. Under different circumstances, all of my relatives would have acknowledged that I, a financial professional with years of experience, was the most qualified person to handle closing an estate. However, there is nothing like a few assets to bring out the worst in a family. In looking back, I marvel at the grace God granted me to withstand all of the negative criticism without developing a root of bitterness. By the time the estate was settled, having heard about numerous court appearances, endless paperwork, incompetent attorneys, and many other frustrations, everybody was relieved that I, rather than they, had been chosen to handle these matters.

If you are currently experiencing a situation where others resent your expertise, understand that you are not the problem. Your family, friends, coworkers, or other detractors are simply responding out of their own sense of inadequacy. Your mere existence and all that you represent threaten them. Recognize and seek to understand their insecurity and make a reasonable attempt to include them in the decision-making process when possible. Most importantly, maintain a positive, humble attitude. Make a conscious decision to forgive them immediately if they criticize you. This is called life. It is the price you pay for being the competent, confident person you are designed to be. Remember that alienation is often the price one pays for his distinction.

> *Remember that alienation is often the price one pays for his distinction.*

Devaluing Others

Someone once said, "No man is a complete failure until he begins disliking men who succeed." I agree wholeheartedly. I have two acquaintances, whom I will call Mary and Sally, who are entrepreneurs in the same service-oriented business. Sally is very professional, renders excellent customer service, and is extremely thoughtful in sending birthday cards to friends and business associates. One day I remarked to Mary what a wonderful person Sally was. Her reply stunned me: "You know she had an affair, don't you?" I knew immediately that her comment sprang from a heart of envy. You see, Sally has a great track record with all of her clients, while Mary's deals always seem to be fraught with misunderstandings and conflict. Being the shy person that I am (not!), I asked her, "Why did you tell me that? Are you trying to make me think less of her?" Of course, Mary denied that was her intention. She said, "No, I just thought you should know that since everybody thinks Sally is so innocent." Who appointed Mary to correct people's perception of Sally?

Ironically, Sally had already told me about her remorse over having the affair and the fact that she had made peace with God concerning it. However, Mary was too envious and insecure to allow any accolades to go to her competitor. She obviously believed that a compliment directed toward Sally was a strike against her value. That is scarcity thinking at its worst. Bishop Charles Blake often says, "Your candlelight won't diminish if you light someone else's candle." We need to get real about our motivation for making disparaging remarks about others. One thing that I have learned is to be honest with myself. David reminds us in Psalm 51:6 that God desires truth in the "inward parts." That is where the healing will start—in the deep recesses of the heart.

There are so many aspects of another person's life that we could envy. If you are ready to be truthful in the inward parts, review the list below and honestly consider if there is a specific individual whom you are envying because of one or more of the advantages or possessions listed. As you name the target of your envy, recall how you have interacted with or discussed this person in the past. Have you ever made critical remarks about her? Now, using a scale of one to ten, ten being highest, go a step further and rate your current level of contentment in each of the corresponding areas of potential envy.

Area of Potential Envy	My Contentment Level (1-10)
Financial Security	_____
Professional Achievements	_____
Intelligence/Education	_____
Physical Attractiveness	_____

Youthfulness/Vitality   _____

Confidence/Assertiveness   _____

Place of Residence   _____

Marital Status   _____

Social Standing/Popularity   _____

Successful Children   _____

Being "Privileged" or Favored   _____

Sophistication/Taste   _____

Other: _____   _____

Having completed this exercise, you may have quickly noticed that the higher your personal satisfaction level in a certain area is, the less likely you are to experience envy in that area. The point of this exercise is to begin to make your envy work for you as a source of revelation and motivation. The key question to ask yourself would be: Is it within the realm of *possibility* for me to obtain the thing that is causing me to envy? Envy is reinforced if you feel you will never be able to achieve the coveted item. Consider *impossible* such things as growing taller, being married to someone else's spouse, changing parents, and so forth. If it is not possible to obtain the coveted item, then settle it in your heart to accept God's plan for your life. If the coveted thing is a possibility, ask yourself the next question: Am I willing to pay the price to obtain it? The world has a saying: "There is no such thing as a free lunch." Everything— except salvation—has a price tag. So, whether you want to be thin, rich, educated, or whatever, your best bet is to stop envying and go toward those who possess what you desire. Find out the secret of their success. Tell them how much you admire them. Indeed you do. Envy is negative admiration! You will find that most people will be flattered and will respond positively to your interest.

CONFIDENCE CHALLENGE

⊛· Within the next few weeks, seek out someone you have envied. Invite her to lunch or dinner at her favorite restaurant (don't forget to pick up the tab) just to "pick her brain" about an area in which she excels. If she is not immediately available, refuse to perceive her response as personal rejection. Remember, you are conquering insecurity. Be patient. Persevere.

The Haman Syndrome

Seeking Significance

Let another praise you, and not your own mouth;
someone else, and not your own lips.

PROVERBS 27:2

RE YOU TRAPPED BY YOUR TRAPPINGS? Have you surrounded yourself with things you feel others will value highly? This would be a normal indulgence for many insecure people. In many instances, they cannot afford their investment in their trappings. To boot, depending on their level of insecurity, they may even be found bragging about these possessions. People who brag about their accomplishments or possessions often doubt they will be accepted based on the personal value they bring to the table. Therefore, they feel they must divert people's attention to something or someone they feel certain others will find impressive.

Such was Haman's plight. King Ahasuerus had appointed him prime minister, making Haman the second most powerful man in all of Persia. He had everything a man could desire: family, friends, favor, fame, and even a fortune. His promotion to this lofty position, however, did not cure his sagging self-esteem and nagging insecurity. Boasting became the norm in his conversations—even at home with his family. Notice his end-of-the-day conversation with his wife and friends.

> Haman boasted to them about his vast wealth, his many sons, and all the ways the king had honored him and how he had elevated him above the other nobles and officials. "And that's not all," Haman added. "I'm the only person Queen Esther invited to accompany the king to the banquet she gave" (Esther 5:11-12).

Me. My. Mine. Notice Haman's self-absorbed conversation. The entire discussion is all about him. The man thrived on the recognition and the power his position afforded him. I have noticed the extreme self-centeredness and self-consciousness of those who have tied their internal security to their "stuff." Like Haman, their conversations revolve only around the things that affect them. Sadly, his boasting revealed his search for significance. But the story gets worse.

King Ahasuerus had ordered everyone to bow in Haman's presence. Everyone. However, when one insignificant Jew, Mordecai, refused to bow, Haman became so angry that he started to plot not only Mordecai's death but also the annihilation of all the Jews. He decided to make a special trip to the palace to get the king's permission to implement his plan.

When he arrived at the palace, however, he did not get a chance to make his request. The king had a pressing matter that needed Haman's attention. As destiny would have it, Ahasuerus had not been able to sleep the night before and had decided to read some of the chronicles of events that had occurred during his 12-year reign. He read that Mordecai had actually saved his life by exposing two men who were plotting to kill him. The king had never expressed any appreciation to Mordecai, not even a thank-you note. Obviously a bureaucratic—but providential—blunder.

Enter Haman. When the king asked him what he would do for a man whom he desired to honor, Haman assumed the king was speaking of him. So he replied,

> If the king wishes to honor someone, he should bring out one of the king's own royal robes, as well as the king's own horse with a royal emblem on its head. Instruct one of the king's most noble princes to dress the man in the king's robe and to lead him through the city square on the king's own horse. Have the prince shout as they go, "This is what happens to those the king wishes to honor!" (Esther 6:7-9 NLT).

In today's terms, what Haman asked for was to be seen in the king's clothes, riding in the king's car, and accompanied by the king's companion. Oh, how honored he would be! Imagine the bragging rights these external trappings would afford him.

Ahasuerus loved this idea. "'Go at once,' the king commanded Haman. 'Get the robe and the horse and do just as you have suggested for Mordecai the Jew, who sits at the king's gate. Do not neglect anything you have recommended'" (Esther 6:10 NLT).

What? Mordecai? Haman was mortified! One cannot describe the humiliation that he suffered as he paraded this insolent, insubordinate Jew through the city square shouting his honor. Afterward, he rushed home dejected and disgusted. This time when he called his wife and friends together to recount the events of the day, there was no bragging about the upcoming private banquet with the king and queen. Events had taken a strange twist. They warned him that, in light of current developments, it seemed as though his days were numbered.

At the private banquet that Haman had anxiously anticipated attending, Queen Esther made the shocking confession of her Jewish roots. She proceeded to tell her husband of Haman's plot to annihilate her people. The king ordered him hanged.

Oh, if only Haman had not been so insecure as to need everyone's acknowledgment and admiration. If only he had ignored Mordecai and focused on the people who had honored him. If only he had ascribed intrinsic worth to himself apart from his position. If only...if only.

Snared by the Trappings

Haman is not alone in his pursuit of significance through external trappings. While many insecure people may not resort to bragging about their possessions and associations, they often invest inordinate amounts of money in designer apparel or other trappings. They name-drop about the important people whose coattails they are riding to significance. Their sense of inadequacy is obvious to even a casual observer.

I am careful not to judge Haman too harshly, for I know that people who live in glass houses should not throw stones. Many years ago I hitched my self-worth to a really sharp two-seat convertible Mercedes-Benz. I had inextricably linked that car to my sense of value. To add insult to injury, this little prestigious headache was in the repair shop almost as frequently as it was at home. It became a real source of friction between my husband and me as I clung to my right to own it. After all, it fit the "image" I felt others had of me as a successful professional. God forbid that I should drive an average car. Even though I could afford the Mercedes and its never-ending repairs, I felt I was being a bad manager of my God-given resources because the car was so pricey to maintain. Nevertheless, I didn't want to disappoint the expectations of the relatives and friends who lived their lives through me, my accomplishments, and my acquisitions.

Finally, I sought the Lord to take the scales from my eyes and to heal me of the insecurity that was at the root of my need for this car. He answered my prayer through a ridiculously huge repair bill totaling several thousands of dollars and an ultimatum from my husband. I sold the car to the mechanic and refused to drive a Mercedes for more than five years. I knew a Mercedes-Benz was known to hold its value and was a good investment under normal circumstances, but I believe God allowed that car to be a thorn in my finances until I got to the point where I didn't need it to validate my worth. When I decided to buy a Mercedes again, the motivation was purely investment driven. This fact alone made the purchase negotiations so much easier. I had the ability to walk away from the deal (and indeed did!) because the need for external validation was gone.

What about you? Are you a victim of the "Haman Syndrome"? Do you feel you have so little intrinsic value that you must make a conscious effort to have others focus on some impressive external trapping? Must you have the king's car, the king's clothes, or the king's companions to feel significant? Do you feel less secure without them?

CONFIDENCE CHALLENGE

- What person, possession, or position have you merged with your sense of worth?

- How would you view your life apart from him or it?

- Ask God to give you the grace to emotionally disconnect from the need to have this person or thing and to know beyond the shadow of a doubt that you have independent, inherent value simply because He created you for a sovereign purpose.

The Diotrephes Syndrome
Preserving Preeminence

*Diotrephes, who loves to have
the preeminence among them,
does not receive us.*

3 John 1:9 nkjv

*H*AVE YOU EVER HAD the distinction of being the "only," the "first," or "one of the few" individuals to accomplish a particular goal or to achieve a certain level of success in your environment? Perhaps you hold an honored or highly esteemed position at your church, workplace, or other social setting. You may even have a reputation for being the most skilled, knowledgeable, or highly regarded person in a particular discipline. Whatever the situation, life atop the pedestal can be a heady experience—until someone comes along and threatens to topple you. The insecure individual will resort to almost any means necessary to protect his position or to preserve his place of preeminence.

Insecurity in the Early Church

The apostle John was eager to spread the gospel and to strengthen the new Christians. He wrote and asked Diotrephes, a New Testament church leader, to allow certain ministers to come and preach at his church. Diotrephes flatly denied John's request. John was extremely disappointed with Diotrephes' response and related the incident to his friend Gaius in a subsequent letter. "I wrote to the church, but Diotrephes, who loves to have the preeminence among them, does not receive us" (3 John 1:9 NKJV). Diotrephes was battling the giant of insecurity. He viewed the traveling ministers as competitors who would threaten his position in his church. Therefore, he not only refused to host them but also slandered them with malicious words. He then proceeded to excommunicate the members who desired to receive them. John cautioned Gaius, "Beloved, do not imitate what is evil, but what is good. He who does good is of God, but he who does evil has not seen God" (verse 11).

Note that John characterized Diotrephes' behavior as "evil" and concluded that he had not "seen" God. In other words, he had not discerned God's divine purpose in the scheme of things. Diotrephes' actions were evil in that he operated in fear rather than faith. For him, the spiritual development of the church paled in comparison to his desire to remain the preeminent one in his environment. He did not stop to realize that favor, promotion, and recognition all come from God.

Insecure Leaders

Insecurity in leadership has always plagued the church. The Pharisees, a sect of the Jews that emphasized strict adherence to the law, found themselves in a similar dilemma when Jesus came on the scene and started working miracles. Let's listen in on one of their council meetings.

> Then the chief priests and the Pharisees called a meeting of the Sanhedrin. "What are we accomplishing?" they asked. "Here is this man performing many miraculous signs. If we let him go on like this, everyone will believe in him, and then the Romans will come and take away both our place and our nation" (John 11:47-48).

What a sad commentary. These frightened, insecure leaders were striving to maintain their positions. Despite the fact that they had read of the coming Messiah for hundreds of years, they did not recognize Jesus as the fulfillment of God's promise. They envied Him so much that they thought it would be best to kill Him. Even Pontius Pilate, the Roman governor who heard their case against Jesus, knew "it was out of envy that the chief priests had handed Jesus over to him" (Mark 15:10).

Far too many pastors live in constant fear that their members will defect to another church or that key leaders will gain too much popularity. Some pastors, in order to ensure loyalty, surround themselves with people who have few opportunities to gain any significance outside of the pastor's realm of influence. Others are so fearful of abandonment that they impose all kinds of onerous rules designed to keep congregants under control. A friend of mine once had a pastor who rarely allowed her to take a vacation. I personally heard a pastor boast that his members never made a major purchase without consulting him. I recently read the bylaws of a church where the pastor required those who planned to be absent for an extended period to place their tithes in an escrow account so that their absence would not affect the church financially. What amazes me about these kinds of situations is that people will continue to follow such leaders. It makes me wonder about their spiritual and mental state.

Servitude is the loss of personal freedom, while servanthood is personally choosing to serve others.

Followers must understand the difference between servitude and servanthood. Servitude is the loss of personal freedom, while servanthood is personally choosing to serve others. When parishioners fail to understand this difference, they set themselves up for pastoral abuse. But keep this in mind: The freedom inherent in servanthood does not negate proper submission to those whom God has put over you to watch over your soul. The Holy Spirit will let you know when the relationship becomes dysfunctional. He can also give you the courage to set proper boundaries.

Ironically, a pastor's controlling behavior often leads to the very thing he is attempting to prevent. Thus, Job's lament becomes the pastor's self-fulfilling prophecy: "For the thing which I greatly feared is come upon me, and that which I was afraid of is come unto me" (Job 3:25 KJV). Pastors must beware. Those who control their congregation or leaders in such a manner have succeeded in surrounding themselves with a group of dysfunctional individuals who will never have the courage to put forth cutting-edge ideas, take initiative, challenge inconsistencies, and keep pastors accountable. Followers will simply perform their assignments in a dutiful manner and wait for direction from the pastor as to what to do next. Why? Because the pastor has taught them that independent, objective thinking is neither desired nor rewarded. Such yes-men may appear to be unquestionably loyal, but at the root of their blind obedience is insecurity. They are deriving their self-worth from being associated with and accepted by the pastor.

Further, for a pastor to promote faith every Sunday but then to live in fear of losing control or losing members is just downright hypocrisy and false advertising. Where is his God, who is in charge of his destiny?

A Modern-Day Example

My husband and I had the wonderful privilege of sitting under the pastoral leadership of the late Dr. H. Marvin Smith at West Adams Foursquare Church in Los Angeles, California. Pastor Marvin was one of the most secure men of God I have ever met. He surrounded himself with several highly capable ministers, including his wife, the late Dr. Juanita Smith. He was never intimidated by any of them, even though some were more charismatic and engaging in their preaching style. He believed and often stated that he was the pastor by the sovereign will of God, period. He did not live in fear of a rebellion, church split, or other common threats that cause pastors so much anxiety. In fact, he used his ministerial staff to help him balance his life.

Despite his love for his congregation and his widely acknowledged "pastor's heart," Pastor Marvin took frequent vacations with his family to places far and near. He would say, "I'm sending my love in my absence." The church never missed a beat—financially or spiritually. He left a legacy of how to keep a ministry in perspective and how to keep a marriage strong. He taught us that our devotion to God was to be first in our lives and that the family, rather than the church, was to be our next priority. He deserves to have his picture in the dictionary next to the word "secure."

Insecure First Ladies

A discussion of insecure pastors would not be complete without addressing the insecurity that plagues many pastors' wives or "first ladies," as they are affectionately called in religious circles. Unfortunately, every first lady lives in the proverbial fishbowl, where critical or opinionated eyes constantly evaluate her every action. Perfection is often the expectation but never the reality. The flirtations of unwise female parishioners starved for male attention can cause the first lady great anxiety. Further, the pastor's naivete or denial of their unholy intentions only exacerbates her insecurity. Meanwhile, she is expected to model peace, joy, and unshakable confidence despite the circumstances. How is she to cope? Consider the following counsel.

She should do her job. She must take care of business at home and leave the rest to God. Rather than her top priority being the traditional oversight over the women's department or other auxiliary at church, the first lady's primary objective must be to minister to her husband. This means being his lover, admirer, and chief supporter. Creating an atmosphere at home he craves to return to each day is a must. Direct and honest communication (versus sulking and pouting) and clearly expressed boundaries and desires are all godly behavior that will safeguard against smoldering issues that can erode relationships. Of course, good food is important too. The pastor should not have to always wait for the ladies of the church to make his favorite dish.

She should not be suspicious of every attractive woman in the church. In my research for this book, I spoke with talented and attractive women who literally swore they had never exhibited behavior that would indicate impure motives toward their pastor. Yet their pastor's wife alienated them and painted them with the same broad brush of suspicion earned by other women with designs on the pastor. For the first lady to suspect the motive of every woman her husband interacts with is clear evidence that she is allowing a spirit of fear to reign in her life.

She should pray. Since fear, the breeding ground for insecurity, is indeed a spirit, it can only be conquered with spiritual weapons. Prayer is the most powerful one in the arsenal. The first lady must pray that God will reveal to her husband the women who have impure motives and that he will have the wisdom to minimize or eliminate his contact with them. And yes, she must also pray that these women will be saved and learn to serve God with a pure heart. She must use godly discretion in deciding when, or if, she is to apprise the pastor of the sisters who are the object of her prayers. She must believe that God will answer her prayers and either change their hearts or send them away. This is the awesome power of intercession; the intercessor functions as an undercover agent. The women prayed for may never know why their mind-set or affections have changed; they simply start to think and feel differently because God has done an inner work.

My friend Billie Rodgers is an awesome first lady. She prays specific Scriptures over her husband, Jim, on a daily basis. She asserts that her intercession is a much better use of her time and energy than trying to figure out who may have designs on her husband.

The first lady must also pray that God will heal her of the hurts, unmet expectations, and other experiences that have brought her to this stage of insecurity.

She should be gracious. As a recipient of God's grace, the first lady must continue to be gracious even to those who do not mean her well. There may come a time when she will have to speak directly to a woman regarding the impropriety of her behavior. Even so, God will give her the right words so that they will have the right impact. I know a pastor's wife who often engaged in some nasty confrontations with other women about their flirtations with her husband. She developed a reputation for being insecure. We must all remember that there is never an acceptable excuse for ungodly behavior. The apostle Paul admonished the Philippians, "Whatever happens, conduct yourselves in a manner worthy of the gospel of Christ" (Philippians 1:27). Of course, to be gracious in these circumstances requires more than sheer determination or a strong resolve; one must have the supernatural empowerment of the Holy Spirit. Finally, the first lady must not wait until she feels positive emotions before she extends grace toward such flirts. As Nike, the sports apparel manufacturer, exhorts, "Just do it!" The desired emotion will follow the behavior.

> *The church is the only place where the playing field gets leveled without regard to education, social standing, or other worldly measures.*

Insecure Laymen

Insecurity is legendary among the laity. Oh, the jockeying for position, recognition, and favor with the pastor that goes on in every church. Just watch the response of existing lay leaders when new people come into the environment and express eagerness to get to work in God's kingdom. Their reaction is more likely to be subtle rejection, quiet alienation, or downright resentment rather than a warm embracing of the newcomer's skills and talents.

Why is there so much contention in this area? We find the painful answer in the reality that the church is the only place where the playing field gets leveled without regard to education, social standing, or other worldly measures. Where else can a person go, who is of little significance in the eyes of the world, and achieve honor or recognition from a significant number of people? This is by no means a put-down, for the church should indeed be the place where one's pedigree and social standing are irrelevant. Many of the people Jesus associated with had no stature in their society. His disciples were common people: fishermen, for example, and even a tax collector. I believe that the church, among its other purposes, was meant to be the great equalizer.

Many times in the church, there are entrenched leaders who hold honored positions simply because of their years of faithfulness to the ministry or to their assigned tasks—despite the fact that they may be ineffective in their performance. Preserving their preeminence, rather than promoting the kingdom of God, becomes their passion. They view talented new workers as a threat, and this can cause them much anxiety. In many instances, these long-term loyalists become roadblocks to effective ministry as they chase away or discourage new workers. Many times they are unrestrained by the pastor, who is too insecure to risk losing their loyalty.

Sole Heir of Your Destiny

I learned a life-changing truth when I assisted a friend who was a party to a lawsuit over a contested will. The deceased had stated in his will that my friend was to be the sole heir of his estate. When the party who was contesting the will was asked why he was doing so, he replied, "It isn't fair that only one person should benefit when there are so many other relatives." After numerous court appearances, the probate judge ruled in favor of my friend and granted her the property—pursuant to the deceased's will. As I reflected on the outcome of the case, I realized a powerful truth. Each of us is the sole heir of the destiny God has willed for us. No one can thwart His plan. Of course, we may face opposition from those who attempt to, but we do so with the confidence that the victory is already ours. The Bible assures us: "For the Lord Almighty has purposed, and who can thwart him? His hand is stretched out, and who can turn it back?" (Isaiah 14:27).

> *Each of us is the sole heir of the destiny God has willed for us.*

CONFIDENCE CHALLENGE

◈· If you have found yourself fearing the loss of your preeminence in a certain situation, first repent for losing your perspective on God's purpose for bringing you into such a position; that is, for His glory—not yours. Second, rest in the knowledge that God has sovereignly willed your destiny; you do not have to compete for it. Finally, resist the urge to compete against others for *their* destiny. Relax and serve the Lord with joy.

The Aaron Syndrome

Pleasing People

*As for me and my house,
we will serve the LORD.*

JOSHUA 24:15 KJV

HERE IN THE WORLD IS MOSES?" That was the question on the mind of each person who had followed him in the Jewish exodus from Egyptian bondage. During the journey to the Promised Land, God summoned Moses to Mt. Sinai to give him instructions and commandments for the people. Thing is, God didn't tell him or the people how long he would be gone. Forty days passed. The last time anybody had seen Moses, he was disappearing into the fog on his way to the top of the mountain. He left Aaron, his people-pleasing brother, in charge.

The multitude grew more restless by the day. Somebody decided that something needed to be done about Moses' absence. Assuming he was never coming back, the people approached Aaron.

> "Look," they said, "make us some gods who can lead us. This man Moses, who brought us here from Egypt, has disappeared. We don't know what has happened to

him." So Aaron said, "Tell your wives and sons and daughters to take off their gold earrings, and then bring them to me." All the people obeyed Aaron and brought him their gold earrings. Then Aaron took the gold, melted it down, and molded and tooled it into the shape of a calf. The people exclaimed, "O Israel, these are the gods who brought you out of Egypt!" (Exodus 32:1-4 NLT).

There. All done. Aaron had pacified their impatience. He had gone along to get along. You will notice in the account of this event that Aaron made not the slightest protest. His fear of the people caused him to cave in very quickly to their evil demand for a god. When Aaron finished making the calf, the people began a wild celebration by worshiping it as their new god.

But wait! Here comes Moses—and boy, is he angry. He sees the wild party in progress and the worshiping of the golden calf. He is so upset that he threw to the ground and broke into pieces the stone tablets on which God had personally written the Ten Commandments. Without seeking any explanation, he "took the calf they had made and burned it in the fire; then he ground it to powder, scattered it on the water and made the Israelites drink it" (Exodus 32:20).

Now it was time to confront his brother.

After that, he turned to Aaron. "What did the people do to you?" he demanded. "How did they ever make you bring such terrible sin upon them?" "Don't get upset, sir," Aaron replied. "You yourself know these people and what a wicked bunch they are. They said to me, 'Make us some gods to lead us, for something has happened to this man Moses, who led us out of Egypt.' So I told them, 'Bring me your gold earrings.' When they brought them to me, I threw them into the fire—and out came this calf!" (Exodus 32:21-24 NLT).

Likely story, Aaron.

Owning Behavior

Have you ever noticed that insecure people do not "own" or take full responsibility for their actions? Aaron knew he had personally fashioned the golden calf with his tooling equipment, yet he lied and claimed that the calf mysteriously came out of the fire. His fear of displeasing Moses caused him to shift the blame onto the people rather than admitting that he too had sinned by catering to their demand.

No one in a position of authority can afford to be so weak that he compromises his moral standards or personal convictions to avoid being unpopular or losing favor.

Aaron's "please disease" resulted in disastrous consequences. Moses instructed the tribe of the Levites to kill more than 3000 rebellious people that day, including some of their own relatives. Afterward, God sent a plague among the people to punish them further.

Years later, after Moses' death, Joshua became his successor and finally led the people into the Promised Land. He was no people pleaser. In fact, he sternly warned the Israelites as they settled in the new territory to make a strong commitment to reject idols and to serve God only.

> But if you are unwilling to serve the LORD, then choose today whom you will serve. Would you prefer the gods your ancestors served beyond the Euphrates? Or will it be the gods of the Amorites in whose land you now live? But as for me and my family, we will serve the LORD (Joshua 24:15 NLT).

Joshua did not walk in fear of man's rejection or disapproval. He let the multitude know in no uncertain terms that he would not be going along to get along.

Fear of Being Alone

When we fast-forward to the time Jesus was on the earth, we notice the same "going along to get along" attitude prevailing among some of the Jewish leaders who really believed that Jesus was indeed the Messiah: "Yet at the same time many even among the leaders believed in him. But because of the Pharisees they would not confess their faith for fear they would be put out of the synagogue; for they loved praise from men more than praise from God" (John 12:42-43). What a tragedy! These men made a conscious decision to choose acceptance over eternal life. The thought of alienation from the group was more than they could bear. According to famed psychologist Abraham Maslow, acceptance is one of the basic human needs. However, when we usurp God's authority and decide it is our personal responsibility to get our acceptance needs met, we are prone to making relational decisions that dishonor Him and thwart His purposes in our lives.

It is inherent in the nature of man to want to be in relationship with others. Society punishes lawbreakers by incarcerating them and separating them from their everyday relationships. Even in prison, the most dreaded form of punishment, other than death, is solitary confinement. Some states are trying to ban it as cruel and unusual punishment. God Himself declared, "It is not good for the man to be alone" (Genesis 2:18). Clearly, God wants us to be in relationship with others. We run into trouble, however, when we decide we must maintain a particular relationship, even at the expense of violating God's principles and mandates or His plan for our lives.

Insecure Parents

All authority figures will pay a price when they fail to exercise tough love or to make the proper hard decisions. Parents must especially be on guard. Those who fear rejection or loss of a child's affection will often go along to get along.

Sadly, many are too insecure to discipline their children because they want to maintain their friendship. Since when did a parent's role include being a friend? If most will be honest, they will admit that they frequently say yes when they should say no to make up for the lack of time they spend with their kids. Of course, we know that in the final analysis, an investment of quality time yields a better payoff in the long-term than anything else a parent can do.

Paradoxically, children will usually end up disrespecting or even resenting a parent who operates in that kind of insecurity. I know a man who is now more than 40 years old and laments that his single-parent mother and his older siblings "spoiled" him by catering to his irresponsibility. Of course, he was a master at manipulating them and making them feel guilty when they tried to deny his frequent requests for loans and other favors. He asserts, however, that by giving in to him, they prevented him from becoming the mature man he could have been much earlier in life. His family never had the courage to exercise the necessary tough love. He now blames them for his being a late bloomer.

CONFIDENCE CHALLENGE

- When was the last time you went along with someone in order to avoid displeasing him?

- What exactly did you fear? What is the worst that would have happened had the thing you feared come to pass?

- Think of one area where you would like to exercise your God-directed judgment in the coming days. Plan to do so without fear of repercussion. Remember that God is in control of every aspect of your life.

The Ahithophel Syndrome

Performing or Perishing

*What does man gain from all his labor
at which he toils under the sun?*

ECCLESIASTES 1:3

DEVELOPED A PERFORMANCE-BASED IDENTITY in the first grade when I learned I could get lots of attention and accolades by excelling in my studies. The encouragement and recognition from my teachers were a stark contrast to the domestic turmoil that pervaded our home. Doing my homework was my refuge and reward. Having the right answers in class boosted my confidence, gave me favor with teachers, and earned me a reputation for being smart. Of course, I never *felt* smart. Rather, I felt that God just kept making exceptions for me. I always prayed He wouldn't stop. He didn't; I graduated valedictorian of my high school class. I performed all the way through college, achieving honors and the admiration of family, friends, former teachers, and other folks. The harder I worked, the more recognition I received. It wasn't until I became an adult that one of my spiritual mentors had the courage to point out that my performance-based existence was neither good nor godly. But by then, my behavior was entrenched.

After I became an established professional, I judged everyone by his work ethic and his ability to understand and excel at his job. I had low regard for clock-watchers and anyone who seemed more interested in socializing than working. My husband and I decided against forming a business together when we saw that we were equally frustrated by each other's work style. When we would work on joint projects in the evenings, he would knock off for bed when he became sleepy. I, on the other hand, felt that one should not stop until the project was done. Darnell is very balanced in his approach to life, so he keeps work in perspective. My attempts to run a guilt trip on him for calling it a day had absolutely no impact. I knew it was going to be a challenge to overcome my workaholism because it is such a socially applauded dysfunction. I wore it like a badge of honor. I didn't even attempt to address the problem for several years. However, fully persuaded that freedom from every bondage is found in the Word of God, I finally went on a search for a performance-based biblical character to see how his behavior impacted his life.

Doing or Dying

Meet Ahithophel, King David's advisor. God had gifted him to give wise counsel. In fact, his advice was so good that it "was as if one had inquired at the oracle of God. So was all the advice of Ahithophel" (2 Samuel 16:23 NKJV). Imagine that. When Ahithophel counseled you, it was as if God Himself had spoken to you. What a great asset to any team.

King David's son, Absalom, decided to stage a coup to dethrone his father. The king had to flee for his life. To make matters worse, Ahithophel defected and joined Absalom's rebellion. King David was devastated when he heard the news, for he knew that his son now had the best possible advisor. He earnestly prayed, "O LORD, let Ahithophel give Absalom foolish advice!" (2 Samuel 15:31 NLT). Unfortunately, God could not answer this prayer, for His "gifts and his call are irrevocable" (Romans

11:29). God does not change His mind once He has given a gift; therefore, He was not going to cause Ahithophel to start giving bad advice. It looked as though God was caught in a divine dilemma. After all, David was His chosen king, a man after His own heart, a man who believed in His promise to subdue all of his enemies. What was God to do? Of course, we know that the all-powerful, all-knowing Father is never without a solution to any problem.

King David decided to send his friend Hushai to feign loyalty to Absalom so that he could thwart the advice of Ahithophel. Sure enough, the plan worked. When Absalom convened his strategy council, Ahithophel advised them to immediately pursue and kill King David while he was tired and weary. There would be no need to kill the loyal soldiers who had followed him. After all, when the shepherd is gone the sheep would scatter (see 2 Samuel 17:1-4). Desiring a second opinion, Absalom asked Hushai what he thought of Ahithophel's plan. Hushai opposed it and presented an alternative strategy. The council accepted it. Absalom and all the men of Israel said, "The advice of Hushai the Arkite is better than that of Ahithophel" (2 Samuel 17:14).

There is probably no greater humiliation to one with a performance-based identity than to be rejected in favor of someone with lesser talent, skills, or reputation.

There is probably no greater humiliation to one with a performance-based identity than to be rejected in favor of someone with lesser talent, skills, or reputation. It would be like a world-renowned actress losing a role to a starlet or a beautiful woman being forsaken for a plain Jane.

One of the great pitfalls of being performance based is that you believe that the time and effort you invest in something makes you the final word on certain matters. After all, you have literally earned your reputation. You worked for it. Now, when maintaining your reputation becomes your life's priority, it can force you into some pretty bizarre behavior.

Ahithophel was reputed as a wise man, but he had convinced himself that he was the wisest of all. For Absalom and his cohorts to prefer the counsel of the less-reputed Hushai was more than Ahithophel's ego could bear. He felt disgraced. He could never face anyone again; life suddenly had no meaning. "When Ahithophel saw that his advice had not been followed, he saddled his donkey and set out for his house in his hometown. He put his house in order and then hanged himself. So he died and was buried in his father's tomb" (2 Samuel 17:23).

It is interesting to note that the strategy that Ahithophel recommended to Absalom was indeed the better one. However, it did not fit God's purpose for this situation. "The Lord had determined to frustrate the *good advice* of Ahithophel in order to bring disaster on Absalom" (2 Samuel 17:14, emphasis added).

Ahithophel failed to understand that God has a season and a reason for all things. This was not the season for his advice. God's purpose was to destroy King David's enemy. Shortly thereafter, Absalom was killed in an encounter with David's army. The king reclaimed his throne. Had Absalom accepted Ahithophel's advice, the story would have had a different ending.

Now, I believe we would all agree that Ahithophel's suicide was an extreme response. However, his suicide is also symbolic of the "death" act that all performance-based people are prone to commit when someone devalues their performance. Death in any form is separation. Sulking, pouting, running away, and withdrawing are all forms of the separation or "relational suicide" we often use to indicate our displeasure with someone for not accepting our input.

When to Say "Okay"

So what if Ahithophel's advice had not been better than Hushai's? No matter how hard we try, we will eventually fail at something. If we didn't, we wouldn't need the Holy Spirit as our helper.

Oh, that Ahithophel would have had the emotional security to just say "okay" to the rejection of his counsel. Being right was his security blanket, and now it had been callously yanked from him with no regard or respect for his well-earned reputation. But suicide? Nothing should be that important. The one thing I have learned over the course of my career is to say "okay" when my advice is rejected—especially when the buck doesn't stop with me. Many performance-based people simply don't understand where their responsibility ends. Knowing that you're right should be its own reward. Ahithophel knew within himself that he had the best plan for achieving Absalom's objective; what he did not know was that it was contrary to God's will. Of course, there is no evidence that he even prayed to find out God's will.

Many performance-based people simply don't understand where their responsibility ends.

Performance-based people don't leave much room for God's sovereign plans. They are too busy "doing" and then judging their worth by their achievements. They have not learned that solitude and meditation could be their most worthwhile endeavors.

The Pitfall of Workaholism

A performance-based individual can work his way right out of the will of God. "But," you may ask, "doesn't God encourage hard work?" Indeed He does—when it is kept in balance. One of Satan's tactics is to take us from one extreme to the other—

from laziness to workaholism. Understanding the difference between being a hard worker versus a workaholic is key. Hard workers have the sense to set limits on how much they will do in the course of a day. They give it their best shot while they are at it. They do not allow work to constantly interfere with their commitments to family and friends. For them, work is simply a means to an end, a necessary endeavor for enjoying the life they want.

On the other hand, a performance-based individual allows his work to define him, which can ultimately lead him into the pit of workaholism. I was in denial about my propensity toward workaholism until I realized that I had too many of the telltale symptoms:

- I worked late the majority of the time.
- Most of my conversations revolved around the issues at the office.
- I rarely took lunch breaks.
- I was always multitasking; I rarely performed any task single-mindedly. If I talked on the phone, I would also use the time to tidy the house. If I watched television, I also organized papers, and on and on it went.
- When I tried relaxing, I would think of all the things I should be doing.
- My to-do list had more items on it than I could possibly achieve during a single day.
- I was a slave to my overcommitted calendar; I left little or no down time.
- Everybody seemed to move too slowly.
- I was always rushing to the next appointment.
- I looked forward to the accolades I received for performing well.
- I found little time to nurture my friendships.

The only relationship that received the proper attention was my marriage. I was afraid God would zap me if I didn't keep it on the front burner. I had excellent mentors early in my marriage whose cautions on wrong priorities constantly echoed in my mind and kept me on track. Besides, my husband is a good communicator who doesn't hesitate to express his expectations, so he always gets his time. I also found time to respond to the never-ending emergencies and needs of my immediate family. Unfortunately, the person who was most deprived of my time was myself. I desperately wanted to get on my own calendar. The idea of "me time" seemed like a fantasy.

I started my road to recovery—which I'm still on—by laying all my activities at the feet of Jesus during my now-extended prayer time. I asked Him to show me what to keep and what to discard. I started resigning from committees, boards, and other activities that were not fitting into my long-term goals. The *decision* to resign was easy but actually giving notice was hard. I felt I had erased something I needed on my résumé—and I wasn't even looking for a job. Some of my involvements were pretty ego enhancing, and I felt I had diminished a little of my significance because I wasn't going to be associated with them any longer. And here I was thinking I had totally conquered my insecurities.

Today, I try to engage in only those activities I feel are a part of God's plan for my life. I am still busier than I'd like to be, but I'm gradually getting control of my schedule. When I recently took a part-time leave of absence from my office, I realized that leisure time is God's idea. He commanded rest and opposed excessive working even when it seemed justified. He admonished the Israelites, "Six days are set aside for work, but on the Sabbath day you must rest, even during the seasons of plowing and harvest" (Exodus 34:21 NLT). Why, that was the busiest time of the year.

Some performance-based folks would have been disappointed with how Jesus responded to His disciples when they came and reported to Him how successful they had been in their ministry tour.

> The apostles gathered around Jesus and reported to him all they had done and taught. Then, because so many people were coming and going that they did not even have a chance to eat, he said to them, "Come with me by yourselves to a quiet place and get some rest" (Mark 6:30-31).

You would have thought that Jesus' first response would have been "Attaboy" or "Keep up the good work." Not so. He knew the importance of rest and He knew the dangers of overengaging in *works*—even the work of ministry.

Performance-Based Spirituality

A performance-based mind-set will usually flow right over into our spirituality. We may start to think we can earn brownie points with God by performing good deeds and other laudable works. But God expects us to do works *because* we love Him and not *so that* He will love us. "He saved us, not because of the good things we did, but because of his mercy. He washed away our sins and gave us a new life through the Holy Spirit" (Titus 3:5 NLT). One of the perils of having a performance-based identity is that we can become legalistic and condemn ourselves and others when we or they fall short of our self-imposed expectations. We may even find that some of our works are not done out of a pure heart to serve. A good test of motive would be to do something good for someone and refuse to mention it to a single soul. Can you forego the recognition and appreciation?

Once we make a decision to set ourselves free from performance prison, we may find that we will be a lot more relaxed and fun to be around. We have to be vigilant in balancing our work, our play, and our spirituality. Since most of us are prone to scheduling our activities, we can use this discipline to bring order to the rest of our daily living. Set your prayer appointment, set your date night with your spouse, set your lunch dates with friends weeks in advance, set a time for recreation with your family, and most of all, set everything according to its importance. Guard the time and do everything possible to keep the appointments.

Even though I feel I have escaped performance prison, I know that if I do not keep my current responsibilities in perspective, I can easily wind back up in lockdown. It is a daily challenge that requires complete submission of everything to my Father's will.

CONFIDENCE CHALLENGE

⊘· Stop and pray right now for the wisdom to know that your value resides simply in the fact that you are a *human being* rather than a *human doing*.

⊘· Meditate on the following passage as you work toward achieving balance in your endeavors.

Whatever I am now, it is all because God poured out his special favor on me—and not without results. For I have worked harder than all the other apostles, yet it was not I but God who was working through me by his grace (1 Corinthians 15:10 NLT).

The Elihu Syndrome

Imagining Inadequacy

Not that we are adequate in ourselves
to consider anything as coming from ourselves,
but our adequacy is from God.

2 CORINTHIANS 3:5-6 NASB

ELIHU SEEMS TO HAVE APPEARED at Job's house out of nowhere. There is no mention of him during the first 31 chapters of the book of Job. Instead, we read of Job's three finger-pointing, so-called friends, who accuse him of causing his own suffering. Having read the story, we know that Satan was behind Job's physical, emotional, and financial afflictions. In chapter 32 of this saga, when the three miserable comforters ceased their lengthy discourses, Elihu decided to speak. It soon becomes apparent that he had been present all along—but he had held his peace. He listened with great patience as Eliphaz, Bildad, and Zophar made their extensive arguments. When Elihu finally spoke, he explained why he had kept silent: "I am young in years, and you are old; that is why I was fearful, not daring to tell you what I know. I thought, 'Age should speak; advanced years should teach wisdom'" (Job 32:6-7).

Elihu was intimidated by the age and experience of Job's friends and assumed they were wiser than he. His imagined inadequacy silenced him. In his eyes, he was not qualified to express an opinion on the cause of Job's suffering. Why, he could not even hold a candle to these icons of wisdom. Therefore, he relegated himself to the listening corner. However, after hearing their long and meaningless discourses, he realized that their perspective on Job's problem was not superior to his. Feeling emboldened, Elihu suddenly knew that he, too, had some ideas that were worth putting on the table. He continued: "But it is the spirit in a man, the breath of the Almighty, that gives him understanding. It is not only the old who are wise, not only the aged who understand what is right. Therefore, I say: Listen to me; I too will tell you what I know" (Job 32:8-10). He spoke nonstop for six chapters. He no longer saw himself as the loser in the game of comparison.

> *When your sense of adequacy rests upon your knowledge bank, you will never tap into the omniscient mind of God.*

When your sense of adequacy rests upon *your* knowledge bank, you will never tap into the omniscient mind of God. You have to accept the reality that you will never know all you need to know for every situation. Elihu's story was made real to me when I had to make a presentation to a large group at a Fortune 500 company where I had just landed a job. I had no previous industry experience and knew that my being hired was a political move by the company. Already feeling insecure in the position, I really went into an emotional tailspin when I was asked to make a special presentation along with two executives who had several years of experience with the company. To boot, one was literally a rocket scientist; the other was a member of Mensa, an elite society of people with extremely high IQs. I, Satan whispered, was a "densa," a term he coined for the really stupid.

During my devotional on the day of the presentation, the Holy Spirit led me to the story of Elihu. I immediately knew that Job 32:8 was my word for the day: "It is the spirit in a man, the breath of the Almighty, that gives him understanding." Relying totally upon God to speak through me, I made the presentation and received great reviews.

The Curse of Comparisons

Feelings of inferiority are not generated by one's mere observation of his condition, but rather by comparing his condition to that of another. Take the case of Suzie, who has always been slightly overweight but not obese. She normally feels pretty good about herself. In fact, she even feels a bit proud when she encounters another woman who is grossly overweight. However, her glorying is short-lived when she meets a woman who is the size she dreams of being. She finds herself eyeing her the entire time she is in her presence. She cannot deny or escape feelings of insecurity that overwhelm her during these times. Comparison is a deadly game that will leave you trapped between the two extremes of inferiority or superiority. Don't play it.

As a Man Thinketh

We must be careful to monitor what we allow to occupy our minds lest it becomes our reality. Can you recall a time when you felt so inadequate that you kept quiet and refused to speak up, even though you had a worthwhile thought or idea? As did Elihu, you must realize that it is not your ability, your knowledge, or your experience that determines your success. The "secret to success" is total dependence on the enabling power of the Holy Spirit. The apostle Paul so aptly stated, "By the grace of God I am what I am" (1 Corinthians 15:10 KJV). Once you become fully persuaded of this fact, you will begin to take on new levels of risk or responsibility without fear of failure. You will have finally understood that God never gives a person a responsibility without giving him the ability to respond. Why not stop, look in the mirror right now, and say to yourself, "When God gives me a responsibility, He gives me the ability to respond!"

Several men in the Bible felt an overwhelming sense of inadequacy when God gave them an assignment that would later cause them to become known as great men. Let's look at a couple of them. Observe their confessed insecurities and the accomplishments they made when enabled by the grace of God.

> *God never gives a person a responsibility without giving him the ability to respond.*

When God charged Moses to lead the Israelites out of Egyptian bondage, Moses immediately apprised Him of his inadequacy for the job. "Moses pleaded with the LORD, 'O Lord, I'm just not a good speaker. I never have been, and I'm not now, even after you have spoken to me. I'm clumsy with words'" (Exodus 4:10 NLT). God would not hear of it. "'Who makes mouths?' the LORD asked him. 'Who makes people so they can speak or not speak, hear or not hear, see or not see? Is it not I, the LORD? Now go, and do as I have told you. I will help you speak well, and I will tell you what to say'" (Exodus 4:11-12 NLT). Despite God's reassurance, Moses still protested. They finally compromised by God agreeing to send Moses' eloquent brother, Aaron, with him to be his spokesperson. Through a series of miracles, God convinced Moses that He was going to be with him every step of the way. Moses became the Great Deliverer.

When God told Gideon to lead the Israelites in the battle against the powerful Midianites, he, too, cited his inadequacy for the job because of certain insecurities he had.

"'But Lord,' Gideon asked, 'how can I save Israel? My clan is the weakest in Manasseh, and I am the least in my family.' The LORD answered, 'I will be with you, and you will strike down all the Midianites together'" (Judges 6:15-16). Gideon went to battle and conquered an army of 135,000 with only 300 soldiers—plus God. That was a ratio of 450 to 1! It takes the presence of omnipotence to achieve those results with limited resources.

> *God delights in exalting those who are inadequate in their own sight.*

I am totally convinced that there are no great men or women, but rather ordinary people who have obeyed God's command to do the extraordinary. God delights in exalting those who are inadequate in their own sight. So the next time Satan reminds you that you are inadequate, agree with him. "You are correct! I am indeed inadequate. However, I am connected to the Supreme Being, who is all-powerful, all-knowing, and always present. Through Him, I can do all things!"

The Real Key to Success

The only real prerequisite for success is obedience. You must exercise faith and show up for the job. Are you ready to be the vessel through whom God can demonstrate His power? If so, He is looking for you. "For the eyes of the LORD run to and fro throughout the whole earth, to show Himself strong on behalf of those whose heart is loyal to Him" (2 Chronicles 16:9 NKJV).

CONFIDENCE CHALLENGE

⌐· What excuse have you made for not pursuing a certain task?

⌐· Do you really think that the excuse is above God's ability to overcome?

PART II

SEVEN ROADBLOCKS TO SUPREME CONFIDENCE

Road·block: An object, situation, or condition that prevents further progress toward an accomplishment

Prayerlessness

Men always ought to pray
and not lose heart.

LUKE 18:1 NKJV

IN THE MOVIE *EXECUTIVE DECISION*, terrorists hijacked a commercial airliner and attempted to divert the flight to another location. Holding only enough fuel for its original destination, the plane soon needed to be refueled. The hijackers, to avoid being subdued on the ground, demanded a midair refueling. A funnel-type device was used to transfer the fuel from the supplying aircraft to the hijacked plane.

As I reflected on the movie, I couldn't help but note the parallel between prayer and the fuel funnel. Prayer, like the funnel, connects us to the source that supplies our every need. Unfortunately, too many people wait until a crisis forces them to make the connection.

The most essential need of the spiritual man is prayer. Prayer is the fuel of the spirit; neglect it and we die spiritually. The problem is that we do not die right away; therefore, we can lapse into extended periods of prayerlessness with no immediate consequences. Some of God's children simply give God a daily wave or a wink as if to say, "I know You are there, but I just have too many things to do to stop and really talk to You. You know my heart though, Lord." Indeed He does.

Prayer: A Life-or-Death Choice

Many years ago there was a popular cigarette commercial on television that featured a smoker sporting a black eye and a cigarette dangling from the corner of his mouth. He would look into the camera and defiantly declare, "I'd rather fight than switch!" The point he was making was that he was committed to doing whatever it took to stay loyal to his brand. The book of Daniel tells us that Daniel had an even stronger commitment to his prayer time (see Daniel 6). Although he had many responsibilities as one of the three administrators over Babylon, Daniel made the time to pray three times a day—and still excelled above the other, very envious administrators. When they learned that King Darius was planning to make Daniel the number two man, they played dirty politics. They convinced the king to sign an irrevocable decree that if anyone prayed to any god or man except the king for a 30-day period, he would be thrown into a den of lions. Darius had no idea this was a trap for Daniel, whom he loved.

Prayer is the fuel of the spirit; neglect it and we die spiritually.

"But when Daniel learned that the law had been signed, he went home and knelt down as usual in his upstairs room, with its windows open toward Jerusalem. He prayed three times a day, just as he had always done, giving thanks to his God" (Daniel 6:10 NLT). Daniel was not willing to submit to prayerlessness—not even for 30 days—to keep his important position or even his life. *He would rather die than switch!*

Sure enough, the administrators finked on him and he was promptly thrown into the lions' den. We read of no distress on Daniel's part, for he had many prayers already stored up for such a time as this. He was secure in his God. He knew that his competence, his career, and his confidence were directly connected to Him.

Daniel also knew the power of prayer. His prayers had bailed him and his friends out of other impossible situations. For example, years earlier Nebuchadnezzar, the then-reigning king, had demanded that Daniel interpret a dream that even Nebuchadnezzar could not remember. The executioners had already started killing the magicians, enchanters, sorcerers, and astrologers who could not meet the king's demand. Rather than hiding, Daniel had gone to the king and requested time to go and pray about the matter, promising to bring him the answer. As expected, God had revealed the details of the dream as well as the interpretation. Daniel came out of prayer giving God the glory. "I thank and praise you, O God of my fathers: You have given me wisdom and power, you have made known to me what we asked of you" (Daniel 2:23). A big promotion had followed for him and his friends.

Meanwhile, back at the lions' den, God sent His angels to deliver a "shut your mouth" order to these kings of the beasts, rendering them harmless. The next morning, to everyone's surprise, Daniel was still alive and well. Darius was so relieved that he ordered the accusing administrators thrown to the lions along with their wives and children. Now, not only did Daniel get the promotion, but the king ordered everyone in his kingdom to fear and reverence Daniel's God.

This story is a powerful reminder that nothing should take priority over our prayers to God. We cannot afford the consequences of prayerlessness. Our confidence and emotional security will come out of maintaining a close connection with Him—and Him alone.

Lessons from My Iron

Like most people during these fast-paced times, I run a pretty tight schedule. For convenience, I always keep my iron and ironing board in the ready position in my closet. One morning I started to press my skirt and quickly noticed that the iron was having no impact on the wrinkles. I glanced down and saw that it was unplugged. I quickly remedied the problem. However, as I stood there impatiently waiting for it to heat up, I realized that sometimes our lives can be very much like my iron experience—a whole lot of effort but no effectiveness. It is only when we plug into our Supreme power source that we become effective.

On another occasion, I was ironing and stepped away for a while to answer the phone. When I returned, the automatic shutoff feature had caused the iron to become cold from inactivity. Even though this frustrated me, I sensed that another spiritual lesson was on the way. The Father reminded me, "Although you may have plugged in to Me some time ago, emotional security, like a fire, must be stoked on a regular basis." The only way to do that is with constant communion with Him. Having prayed, we can begin, by faith, to behave and to believe like a secure person.

The Behavior of the Remora Fish

I am often amazed at the spiritual lessons found in the wonders of nature. The remora, for example, provides a powerful model of the importance of staying connected to a source bigger and more powerful than ourselves. This fish has an oval sucking disk on the top of its head that allows it to attach itself to the underside of other large fish or sea vessels. The shark is its favorite host target.

Once attached to the shark, the remora does not have to concern itself with daily issues such as food, transportation, or safety. It feeds on the food that falls from the shark's mouth. Of course, it has the option of swimming on its own, but when it decides to attach to the shark, it goes where the shark goes. It does not attempt to go in a direction contrary to the shark. Protection? It is a nonissue for one who is connected to such a powerful and fearless creature. The remora is secure. It innately knows the shark can carry it to places it could never go alone.

Doesn't this sound like the relationship God desires for His children to have with Him? He wants us to feed on the words that come out of His mouth. He wants us to go with Him where He leads and not to take off on independent excursions, hoping He will tag along. He wants us to live with the assurance that He will protect not only our lives, but also our relationships and all that pertains to us. Oh, that we would emulate the remora. We would then find ourselves securing our attachment to God on a daily basis through prayer. He is waiting to carry us to places we fear to go alone.

The prophet Isaiah admonished the Jewish leaders to "pray to the LORD day and night for the fulfillment of his promises. Take no rest, all you who pray. Give the LORD no rest" (Isaiah 62:6-7 NLT). Are you giving God too much rest?

My Prayer Model

Prayer is often talked about, but of the spiritual disciplines, it is probably one of the least-practiced. Many of God's children claim that prayer is their top priority. Perhaps it is in *theory*. However, a person's *real* priority is the activity in his life that takes precedence over all others. I was blessed to be mentored by people who made prayer an important part of their lives. I remember foregoing summer vacations in my early twenties to travel to Philadelphia, Pennsylvania, to spend time daily at the altar with Dr. Marlene Talley, Dr. Elvin Ezekiel, and their group of dedicated Christians young and old who were passionate about prayer.

Even as a young woman I had long wanted to teach on the subject but knew I was not really modeling the precepts I wanted to teach. It seemed I had allowed my extremely busy schedule to crowd out what I really desired to be my priority. My friend P. "Bunny" Wilson reminded me that a teacher is most effective when she practices the principles she preaches. Bunny admonished me, "You can talk about it, but you can't teach it." She challenged me to take my prayer life to another level. I accepted her challenge.

Being a schedule-driven person, I have found I am more consistent when I set an appointment in advance to spend time with God. Further, since I tend to do better with structure, I need a prayer tool that keeps me focused. Using the word "pray" as an acronym, I developed and now follow the guidelines below during my prayer time.

Pause. I stop all activity and focus completely on God. Worship is total preoccupation; we can only be preoccupied with one thing at a time. I know that many people pray while they exercise or drive to work. However, the greatest honor and respect we can give to anyone is our undivided attention. After all, we come into His presence to worship Him. I sit, stand, or kneel in silence. I breathe deeply and slowly. With each breath I absorb His presence, His holiness, and His power. I have my prayer journal and a pen ready to record His thoughts to me throughout the time of prayer.

Reverence. I give Him honor and admiration. I hallow (make sacred; bless) His name. At this point, distractions start to pop up like dandelions. I will notice a dead leaf on a houseplant or something out of place in the room, or I will suddenly remember a task I need to put on my to-do list. I jot down the task in my journal and ignore the other issues for what they are—mere distractions that can be dealt with later. I have also learned that praying audibly helps to minimize wandering thoughts. When I am extremely tired or sleepy, I walk around while praying rather than kneeling. You can't be so spiritually minded that you do not deal with the practical issues of the flesh. Fatigue is real.

I come into His presence singing songs that exalt Him. I thank Him for all He has done and will do. I express several things I am particularly grateful for that day. I read and meditate on a passage of Scripture. I recommend that beginners read a chapter in the life of Jesus from one of the four Gospels, or a chapter from the book of Proverbs that corresponds with the date of the month (there are 31 chapters). Further reading options may include a chapter from the book of Acts, noting the power of the early church, or a psalm. I personally enjoy studying particular subject matters, such as faith, forgiveness, pride, and so forth.

Ask. I ask for forgiveness of my sins, making every effort to be specific. I pray for the power to live a Christian life and ask God to give me a passion for His Word and for prayer. I ask for His will to be done in every aspect of my life: spiritually, physically, financially, relationally, vocationally, and emotionally. I pray for each one separately.

Using a prepared list, I ask for God's will to be done in the lives of my family members; friends; coworkers; neighbors; pastor/church; national, state and local government; and others. Rather than launching into a "let it be…" mode, I ask the Holy Spirit to make intercession for me according to the will of God. By the way, that is His job according to Romans 8:26-27: "In the same way, the Spirit helps us in our weakness. We do not know what we ought to pray for, but the Spirit himself intercedes for us with groans that words cannot express. And he who searches our hearts knows the mind of the Spirit, because the Spirit intercedes for the saints in accordance with God's will."

Yield. When all is said and done, I know I must subordinate my requests to God's sovereign will, trusting that He knows what is best. I strive to maintain a "nevertheless" attitude toward all of my requests. Therefore, I am careful to conclude my prayer by saying, "Nevertheless, not my will, Lord, but Yours be done." Now, I must admit that sometimes the devil tries to make me feel that I am being hypocritical by saying "nevertheless" since

I do indeed, in the natural, often prefer a certain outcome. Notwithstanding, my regenerated heart desires the perfect will of God. Therefore, I thank Him in advance for granting my petitions according to *His* wisdom and foreknowledge.

I leave the prayer room knowing I have made the connection and have been refueled. My knowing is not based upon any special emotions or chills that I feel but simply on the fact that God is always listening to the prayers of His children.

There is an adage that asserts that it is not *what* you know but *whom* you know that gives you the advantage in a situation. I agree wholeheartedly from a spiritual point of view. When we have a relationship with God, we come to understand that He is sufficient to handle any demand placed upon us. That kind of confidence comes from knowing we are connected to omnipotence.

CONFIDENCE CHALLENGE

- Make a formal written commitment to be faithful to a daily time of prayer for at least a certain number of minutes during a certain number of days per week.

    Sample Commitment: "With the help of the Lord, I commit to 20 minutes of prayer for five days per week for the next 30 days."

- Throughout each day, pause for a simple five-second praise or thanksgiving declaration. For example:

    "Lord, I thank You that You are with me."
    "Father, You are awesome."
    "Thank You for Your wisdom."

"Thank You for the angels You have given charge over me and my family."

"Lord, nothing is too hard for You."

"Thank You for life, health, strength, and a sound mind."

"There is none like You in all the earth."

ROADBLOCK 2

Personal Devaluation

She perceives that her merchandise is good.

PROVERBS 31:18 NKJV

WOMEN AND MEN HAVE BATTLED feelings of inadequacy ever since the beginning of time. Eve, in spite of her perfect surroundings in the Garden of Eden, allowed the serpent to convince her that she was inadequate in knowledge and needed to eat the forbidden fruit.

Mental health professionals and self-proclaimed life coaches, as well as popular clergy, have offered various solutions to the dilemma of low self-evaluation—only to find that it is still one of mankind's most common problems. The perception of personal inadequacy persists because of our inadequate understanding of the role God is to play in our lives.

Money and Mankind

In many ways, the worth of a person can be compared to the value of money. Assume, for example, that you have a $100 bill that is worn, torn, and otherwise disfigured. The fact that it is no longer new and crisp does not diminish its value. No matter how it looks, its value remains unchanged simply because it was established by its maker; that is, the U.S. government. It will always be worth $100 and can be used to purchase whatever any $100 bill normally purchases. A customer in any establishment would become extremely upset if he presented a well-worn $100 bill to pay for his goods or service and the merchant responded, "Sorry, I can only give you $50 of value because your currency is battered and torn." The customer would conclude that the merchant was nuts.

There is something on every single bill of currency that makes it different from any other—its serial number. No other bill has that number. In fact, I once proved that a cash clerk was stealing from the company when I photocopied and then planted some currency in the incoming mail. Within an hour of her suspected theft, I confronted her and asked to see the money in her purse. She vehemently denied that it was the company's money. When I compared the serial numbers of her bills to that of the planted money, they matched perfectly. Her defense was shot. You see, until then, she was not aware of the fact that each bill had a unique identity.

God established our value when He created us. He made each one of us unique. We honor Him when we embrace our uniqueness. Also, just as the government creates currency bills with various denominations, God created us with the variety we need to fulfill our designated purpose. We all have a unique value and different destiny. Before He created each of us, He had a plan that called for our lives to be spent according to His sovereign plan.

Lessons from the Virtuous Woman

The nameless superwoman described in Proverbs 31:10-31 has been the subject of many sermons. In this narrative, King Lemuel's mother is giving her son advice regarding the character traits and behavior patterns that he should look for in the woman he planned to marry. I find verse 18 particularly encouraging for those who battle insecurity: "She perceives that her merchandise is good" (NKJV). Let's look at five liberating truths found in this simple phrase.

1. *She* perceives that her merchandise is good. She is not one who comes to the table looking for validation or approval of her wares. When one is insecure and does not personally value what she brings to the table, others may be able to minimize it or convince her that it does not rate. This woman, like all humans, desires acceptance and validation, but she will not seek it or find herself debilitated if she does not get it.

2. The ideal woman *perceives* that her merchandise is good. To perceive is to sense, know, or understand inwardly. She understands what she brings to the table and she inwardly values it. She will not doubt the value of its worth; neither will she find it necessary to brag about the quality of her merchandise. The ideal woman will not have her nose turned up in pride, but neither will her eyes be cast down with false humility. She simply has a balanced view of her wares. Notice that she does not pretend that her merchandise is good, for it is hypocritical and difficult to attempt to fake confidence. The facade will soon become evident to the discerning person. No, Mrs. Proverbs 31 simply perceives the worth of her wares. Beware. Even if you have the utmost confidence, someone may still attempt to minimize your worth and say that what you bring is of little or no value—but their opinion will not faze you when you are fully persuaded on the inside, when you perceive your value.

3. She perceives that *her* merchandise is good. Here is a woman who is not intimidated by or unduly concerned about the goods of the other merchants. Consequently, she doesn't spend her energies comparing or competing. Her merchandise speaks for itself. As a Christian, competing for anything in life outside of the area of sports is as pointless as trying to outrun another car on the freeway. Both drivers have a different destination. Why should you compete with another person for your

destiny when God has already ordained it? I find great encouragement in the psalmist's reminder, "All the days ordained for me were written in your book before one of them came to be" (Psalm 139:16).

4. The verse states that she perceives that her merchandise *is* good. This woman has current confidence. She is not stuck in the past, thinking about the good merchandise she used to have. Neither is she postponing the pursuit of her goals until her merchandise is perfect. She simply steps out in faith, having done the best she could. Her merchandise is good today; tomorrow is in God's hands. Anxiety has no place in her life.

5. This mentally and morally strong woman perceives that her merchandise is *good*. She embraces and values what she brings to the marketplace. She refuses to allow man, media, or merchants to define or set the standard for her merchandise. You see, your merchandise is whatever you offer to the world. It could simply be a positive attitude, integrity, confidentiality, loyalty, or any other intangible quality. And, although society may not set a great store by it or grant you special recognition because of it, you must perceive within yourself, as part of your personal, biblically based value system, that your merchandise is good.

Further, there really is no need to feel inadequate around *anybody* when you have an intimate relationship with the One who created *everybody*. Someone once said, "He who kneels before God can stand before anyone."

CONFIDENCE CHALLENGE

⁊· What merchandise do you bring to the table? Do you really perceive that it is good?

⁊· From the list of intangible qualities below, see how many you can circle as your own "good merchandise." Feel free to add other qualities to the list.

> affectionate, approachable, articulate, assertive, confidential, considerate, dependable, determined, discerning, disciplined, discreet, decisive, encouraging, even-tempered, flexible, finisher, generous, genuine, good listener, gracious, hardworking, honest, humble, loyal, organized, objective, peaceful, prompt, sociable, spiritually minded, submissive to authority, supportive, sympathetic, tenderhearted, thorough, thoughtful, thrifty, transparent, truthful, understanding, wise

⁊· Even if you circled only one word above, know that you bring something valuable to the table. Daily declare, "I perceive that my merchandise is good!"

Poor Knowledge

*My people are destroyed
from lack of knowledge.*

HOSEA 4:6

"KNOWLEDGE IS POWER" is an adage we have all come to accept as conventional wisdom. The more you know, the more confident you will be, naturally and spiritually speaking. There is nothing that generates a sense of insecurity or inferiority more than inadequate knowledge.

People will go to great lengths to keep from appearing unknowledgeable. You may have had the experience of talking to certain people and discerning from the look in their eyes that they were not comprehending the subject matter, but rather than saying so, they simply nodded. Well, I confess that I have done the same thing a time or so in my life, knowing that I did not have a clue about what the person was saying. God forbid that I should have appeared ignorant! My seven-year-old niece, Allexa, sets a great example for me. When I use a word or make a statement that she does not understand, she quizzes me immediately with, "What does that mean?" If we would stop putting a facade over our occasional ignorance, we would increase our knowledge base even more. Mrs. Scales, my high school English teacher, often reminded her students, "What you don't know will make a whole new world."

Because I will never know everything, I try to enhance the self-esteem of others by allowing them to shine while I learn. I love picking people's brains about their life experiences. It was the British statesman Benjamin Disraeli who declared, "The more extensive a man's knowledge of what has been done, the greater will be his power of knowing what to do."

Secular Knowledge

If "knowledge is power," then what naturally follows is: "Lack of knowledge is powerlessness." What you don't know will hurt you. Those with inadequate knowledge will be powerless to compete for top wages and promotions. This sense of powerlessness only deepens one's sense of insecurity.

Basic survival skills today, and even more so in the future, will require adequate knowledge in the areas discussed below.

Vocabulary skills. Let's face it. People most often judge your intelligence, education, and ability to succeed by how well you speak and the extent of your vocabulary. Numerous studies have shown that there is a direct correlation between vocabulary and income levels.

During my career in corporate America, I witnessed individuals with less technical competence gain the edge over their coworkers because of their strong command of the English language. Developing verbal and written communication skills, whether through formal classes or self-study, is one of the greatest confidence-building endeavors one could undertake. The respect that it engenders is amazing. It enhances a person's sense of security to know that he can hold his own in any group and communicate effectively without searching for words. Gaining skills in this area can be done easily and conveniently through Internet sites, word-a-day calendars, tapes, and books.

I know a woman who is so insecure with respect to her perceived inability to speak correctly that she constantly reads grammar books. She is scared stiff to speak at her church. I have attended church services with her on several special occasions and marveled at the fact that her peers speak frequently—even though they are not as verbally adept as she. They split infinitives and mispronounce words with no apparent embarrassment or insecurity. To boot, they do so in a loud voice—which they equate with "the anointing" or being "in the Spirit."

Now, even if she were to learn every single rule of proper grammar, she would still feel inadequate because she has not turned off that 30-year-old tape of her abusive former husband telling her that she is stupid and inadequate to perform any undertaking. Therefore, she lives in her own mental prison of poor knowledge.

Technical competence. While your vocabulary may get you in the door, sooner or later you must be able to perform. Microsoft billionaire Bill Gates predicts, "There will be 'two societies' in the future: high-paid knowledge workers and low-paid service workers." If you know (or think) your skills are less than par, your confidence is going to sag. Competence equals confidence.

When the woman of Proverbs 31 went out to bargain with the world, she knew she was bringing good merchandise to the table. I believe one of the key reasons she was so confident about her merchandise is found in verse 18, "Her lamp does not go out at night" (NKJV). She puts in the time and exercises the diligence necessary to be excellent in her endeavors.

I taught an accounting class for several years at a large university. It was always apparent which students had studied or done their homework. The prepared ones would stride right to the front of the classroom and take a seat. They had no fear of my calling on them. They had an aura of confidence and the look that comes with being prepared.

Social skills. My husband and I attend many formal banquets. I am often amazed by the number of people who have very little knowledge of proper dining etiquette. They look around, apprehensively waiting for others to start eating so they can follow their example. Inspired by their lack of confidence, I developed a wallet-sized "Confident Dining" card that displays a correct table setting on one side and a list of the top rules of dining etiquette on the other. I see the enlightened look on my customers' faces as they read it, though many claim, "I'm buying this for a friend." Yeah, right.

You need to be socially savvy enough to make proper introductions, to tip correctly, and to demonstrate other indications of fine breeding. Such behavior can have a positive impact on your career as well as your social life. The key thing is to remember to use your skills when needed and not to be a stiff bore when the situation calls for more relaxed behavior. No need to eat that hot dog with a knife and fork at the annual picnic.

True Confidence

Being excellent in your undertakings builds your confidence. Knowing that your skills are honed and that you have done your very best does wonders for your sense of adequacy. Because I strive to excel at whatever I do, I walk in a high level of confidence. Let me explain.

The root meaning of the word "confidence" is "inspiring." The prefix "con" means "with" and the root "fid" means "faith." To walk in confidence is to walk with faith. We can walk with the faith and conviction that we are enabled by a God who knows everything, is all-powerful, and is always present.

The Cost of Confidence

Unfortunately, sometimes when you exude confidence, an insecure person will accuse you of being proud or haughty. You must be careful of the spirit in which you exhibit your confidence so that there is not even a modicum of truth to such an accusation. God forbid that we should believe our own press.

I heard that students in a psychology class at a certain college were asked to name their most valuable asset. Two of them wrote intelligence and both misspelled it. I spoke at a conference once where the theme included the word "excellent." The conference banner displayed a glaring grammatical error.

Inferior by Consent

I worked with a wonderful Christian woman whom I loved dearly and with whom I sincerely desired a close relationship. One morning she told me that several people had told her that I had said she was incompetent. She said this had caused her such emotional pain and resentment toward me that she was not even able to take communion. I felt really sorry for her because Satan had convinced her to believe such a lie. Since I had little or no interaction with her on a regular basis, I had no basis to judge her personal competence. I knew that the people who had told her the lie were speaking their own opinion but had used my name to give their comments credibility. Of course, if she had not inwardly believed on some level that she was incompetent, the lie would have had minimal impact on her. Eleanor Roosevelt said, "No one can make you feel inferior without your permission." Satan, with this woman's consent, had successfully reinforced her insecurity and robbed her—and me—of a potentially wonderful relationship. Why, if someone were to call me incompetent, I would merely shrug it off as his erroneous and envious opinion. I perceive that my merchandise is good. That's not cockiness. That's confidence.

Enough Knowledge

In this current age of information overload, it is impossible to keep up with all of the news and developments on a worldwide or even local basis. Everyone has to find his own comfort zone as to how much information he wants to acquire. I have made a conscious decision to be knowledgeable only in the areas that relate to my current life focus or to specific matters within my circle of concern. Beyond that, I have resorted to reading the "Highlights" and "Opinion" sections of the Sunday paper and listening to an all-news television channel when dressing or cooking. I am content having just enough knowledge to ask reasonably intelligent questions about matters of no real significance to me. I have no need to be a "walking information booth" or to be an icon of wisdom on every subject. Am I advocating an "ignorance is bliss" philosophy? Of course not. I am practicing being secure enough to learn from others. Further, I have found that people will consider you a sparkling conversationalist when all that you have done is asked them questions or allowed them to talk about their favorite subject—themselves.

Notwithstanding, it does wonders for your confidence to be able to converse about a broad range of topics. Again, each person must decide the extent to which he wants to invest the time to secure a large knowledge base. If you are a talk show host, a politician, or work in any other profession where you need to have your finger on the pulse of the world, then delve into the reading material. If not, skim the headlines.

Spiritual Knowledge

Believing that knowledge is power is an even more dynamic truth in the spiritual realm.

The satisfaction of acquiring secular knowledge pales in comparison to the emotional security one can achieve from knowing God and His Word. Proverbs 2:6 is a great reminder: "For the LORD gives wisdom; from his mouth come knowledge and understanding."

The more you know about the promises of God, the more confident you'll be. Even if you never become proficient at the secular skills previously discussed, you can still walk in Supreme confidence because real confidence is achieved by connecting with God.

Knowledge of God's Word can give clarity to the puzzling issues of life. When a certain religious sect tried to pull Jesus into one of their debates on a particular issue, He replied, "Your problem is that you don't know the Scriptures, and you don't know the power of God" (Matthew 22:29 NLT). There are some truths we need to settle in our hearts and let them bring peace to our spirits. For example, I have settled in my heart that, according to Isaiah 14:27, no one can thwart the purpose God has for my life. I have also settled in my heart that, according to Romans 8:28, no matter what happens, things are working out for my good; therefore, I resist anxiety and worry. Because of my knowledge of the Scriptures, I have also decided that, as an act of my will, I will choose to forgive offenses perpetrated against me so that I can be emotionally free to enjoy my life.

My ongoing prayer is that God will keep aflame my hunger for His Word. Following Solomon's admonishment to "buy the truth" (Proverbs 23:23), I have invested in every possible Bible study aid I can find from software to books and Bibles to assure full access to and understanding of God's Word.

Daniel reminds us that God "gives wisdom to the wise and knowledge to those who have understanding. He reveals deep and secret things; He knows what is in the darkness, and light dwells with Him" (Daniel 2:21-22 NKJV).

Yes, the "light," the revelation of the knowledge that we need, does indeed belong to God. We never have to feel insecure regarding any aspect of our knowledge when we know Him, who knows everything.

CONFIDENCE CHALLENGE

⊘· Knowledge is power and ignorance is a choice. Choose to be knowledgeable.

⊘· List, in order of importance to you, the areas of your life (example: spiritually, vocationally, financially, socially, etc.) where you need to enhance your knowledge. State exactly what you feel you need to learn. What resource will you employ to gain the desired knowledge? When will you start? Whom will you solicit to hold you accountable?

Purposeless Living

"For I know the plans I have for you," declares the L<small>ORD</small>,
"plans to prosper you and not to harm you,
plans to give you hope and a future."

J<small>EREMIAH</small> 29:11

O YOU HAVE A CLEAR SENSE of why God put you on the earth, or are you driving aimlessly on life's highway with no destination in mind? A purposeless existence is a major roadblock to emotional security. How can you walk with Supreme confidence and the complete assurance that God will cause you to succeed in your endeavors if you do not know for certain that you are on His path? Sadly, this is the state of too many of God's children. They are not absolutely sure of their purpose for being born. Therefore, they trudge through their daily routines unfulfilled and often completely frustrated with their lack of direction. This is not the "abundant life" Jesus promised in John 10:10 (N<small>ASB</small>).

The Energy of Purpose

Nothing is more gratifying than pursuing one's purpose—even when opposition seems unbearable or other distractions threaten to overshadow it. There is a passion, a fire that refuses to be quenched when you lock into God's plan for your life.

As a financial executive for more than 30 years, it seems that every position I have held in the corporate world has been highly stressful and required me to work overtime. However, I am also fully persuaded that I was put on this earth to model and to teach—through speaking and writing—the principles of financial, as well as relational, freedom. Many times after a long and demanding day, I come home at night feeling brain-dead. It seems, however, that even when I am the most fatigued, I experience a surge of energy and excitement as I sit down to my computer and begin to write the revelations of God. The Scriptures seem to come alive with practical application. In those moments, I know beyond a shadow of a doubt that I am walking in my divine purpose. The fulfillment and personal satisfaction I feel are indescribable.

Because walking in our purpose is so energizing, it seems that if one is in doubt about what his purpose is, a key question he would ask himself would be, "What energizes me and how can I use this energy to improve the life of others?" Surely, everyone has some level of passion for something. Of course, I have talked to people who say they don't have a passion for anything. I believe what they really mean is that they don't have the faith to believe they could actually do what they really desire in their hearts.

The Humility in Purpose

Jesus was a perfect example of what it means to walk in divine purpose. "Jesus knew that the Father had put all things under his power, and that he had come from God and was returning to God; so he got up from the meal, took off his outer clothing, and wrapped a towel around his waist. After that, he poured water into a basin and began to wash his disciples' feet, drying them with the towel that was wrapped around him" (John 13:3-5).

Jesus was keenly aware of three things: First, He knew the source of His *power*. Jesus did not come to earth touting His self-confidence. He knew and often declared that God empowered Him to do all that He did. He admonished us to remember that apart from God we can do nothing. Second, He knew His *purpose*. He had come to seek and to save the lost. Finally, He knew God's *plan* for achieving that purpose. He would work miracles that would cause many to believe, and He would ultimately have to face the cross.

Once you are persuaded of your divine purpose, you can readily humble yourself and serve others without fear that you will be disadvantaged or diminished in the process. Jesus easily washed His disciples' feet without feeling that it took away any of His glory. After all, He would soon be returning to all of the honor and splendor He had enjoyed in heaven before He came to earth.

Jesus didn't worry that someone would upstage Him; He didn't compete with anyone—not even the devil. Like Jesus, we must believe in our hearts that promotion and exaltation come from God, period. No one can steal our divine destiny. Why not? "For the LORD Almighty has purposed, and who can thwart Him? His hand is stretched out, and who can turn it back?" (Isaiah 14:27).

Living in Your Lane

When driving the freeways, we often see a sign that says "Trucks Only." We immediately know that a certain portion of the highway has been set apart to: 1) facilitate the passage of large trucks and 2) avoid impeding the progress of cars. Consequently, all vehicles can reach their destination faster with each staying in their respective lanes. That's how it is when you become secure in your purpose. You become comfortable in your lane. You don't get caught up trying to follow the exact path of others. You don't exit on Main Street just because it's the route Mary takes to her destination. You begin to understand that your purpose may be found on Back Street. Boy, have I learned this lesson.

I grew up in a denomination that embraced a highly emotional delivery style in its preaching. The louder someone spoke, the more the crowd would respond. I also observed that occasionally someone would come to our church who was a teacher and whose delivery was enlightening but without extreme emotion. The people did not respond as well because they had been conditioned to "high-volume" preaching. Well, knowing God had called me to be a teacher, I would cringe whenever I received an invitation to speak at churches in my denomination. When I would get up to speak, I would always apologize before I got started by saying, "Now, I'm *just* a teacher, so you probably won't shout today…" This was my not-so-subtle way of getting them to abandon any expectations that I would be yelling at the end of the message. I felt much more comfortable at churches where the pastor's style mirrored my own. My husband always encouraged me to just be myself but my insecurity in this area blinded me to the fact that the increasing number of calls to speak came from referrals from past engagements. Clearly, someone must have deemed my teaching beneficial.

Not understanding one's purpose can be a major roadblock to emotional security. Had I known I was already walking in divine purpose even in my delivery style, I would have felt no need to apologize. I now realize that my teaching style, consistent with God's teaching gift, is the "lane" He has ordained for me. I don't have to emulate anyone's style. God knows what His children need, and many of them are simply more receptive to particular styles of speaking. If a speaker chooses to "honk the horn" while he is driving, there is no need for me to do so just because it seems to get everyone's attention. As in the truck example cited earlier, I have to respect what he does in his lane rather than be critical of him.

Jesus stayed in His lane and refused to let anyone pull Him away from His primary purpose. One day while He was teaching,

He was interrupted. "Someone in the crowd said to him, 'Teacher, tell my brother to divide the inheritance with me.' Jesus replied, 'Man, who appointed me a judge or an arbiter between you?'"(Luke 12:13-14). In essence, Jesus was saying, "Look, I'm not about to get distracted by conducting an arbitration hearing between you two. That's not part of My purpose for being here on earth."

> *Just because we are capable of performing a task doesn't always mean God is calling us to do it.*

Now, I have to confess that I find it hard to resist the temptation to become involved in matters that are not part of what God has called me to do. In the past I have often rescued people to their detriment—and mine. I am still learning to distinguish between "can" and "call." Just because we are capable of performing a task doesn't always mean God is calling us to do it.

Even up to the day that Jesus gave His life on the cross, there were still many sick people who needed healing, bound people who needed deliverance, and a myriad of other impossible situations that needed His attention. He knew that through the power of His death and resurrection, all could be addressed. So, despite unresolved problems, He confidently gave His heavenly Father this report on his ministry: "I brought glory to you here on earth by doing everything *you* told me to do" (John 17:4 NLT, emphasis added). He refused to let Satan, His disciples, well-meaning family members, needy people, or anyone else distract Him from His purpose.

CONFIDENCE CHALLENGE

- Can you state your divine purpose in a single sentence? Are you ardently pursuing it?

- If you don't yet know what it is, consider whether you are approaching your search from the perspective of how it will enhance *your* life rather than the lives of others.

ROADBLOCK 5

Past Transgressions

If our hearts do not condemn us,
we have confidence before God.

1 JOHN 3:21

WE ARE THE SUM TOTAL of everything we have ever experienced—the good and the bad. We can engage in wishful thinking and imagine that our past negative behavior had never occurred, or we can decide to accept the reality of the experience. How we choose to respond to the past will determine our destiny.

We all have sinned. In so doing, we either responded by asking for God's forgiveness and going forward with the faith that we would not have a repeat performance, or we are still stuck in guilt—always remorsefully reminded that we have done something wrong. Guilt can cause a great deal of insecurity. In the chapter on the "Saul Syndrome" we discussed how Saul's jealousy caused him to seek David's life, for Saul feared David would take his place as king. Saul's insecurity was well grounded. God had already sent word that because of Saul's disobedience, the kingdom was going to be torn from him and given to another. Many times when we know we have not done what we should or have been remiss in our responsibilities, we develop anxiety about possible consequences. For instance, many men and women are plagued with jealousy because of their own infidelity or prior indiscretions. They live in great fear that one day they will reap what they have sown. Some have even resorted to verbal and physical abuse of their partner in order to ward off what they feel will be the inevitable. Take the story of someone whom we will call Sarah.

Sarah had an affair with a married man many years ago and now lives with the nagging fear that her husband will one day violate their marriage vows. She is suspicious of most of the women who interact with him. Her insecurity has not gone unnoticed by friends and acquaintances. Further, because Sarah violated God's law as well as her own sense of morality, she is anxious about the punishment she feels she deserves. She has confessed to me that this keeps her in a state of anxiety and insecurity. How can Sarah break free of her dilemma? She needs to ask for and accept God's forgiveness. This sounds simple, but we all know that it is not easy. It takes faith to accept God's forgiveness and to release ourselves from guilt and condemnation. When we repent, we must *believe* His promise: "Their sins and lawless acts I will remember no more" (Hebrews 10:17). God doesn't remember confessed sin, so we need to stop rehearsing it. God does not want to hear about it ever again. He clarifies, "Now when sins have been forgiven, there is no need to offer any more sacrifices" (verse 18 NLT). Once is enough. There is no need to repent after the first time. To do so is to offer another sacrifice. Too many people sacrifice the rest of their lives on the altar of remorse over a single transgression. Years ago "That's dead" was

> *Too many people sacrifice the rest of their lives on the altar of remorse over a single transgression.*

a popular expression among the young and hip. What they meant by it was that the issue or situation was of no more importance or consequence. When God forgives you and the devil comes back to remind you of your past transgression, respond with a shout, "That's dead!"

It is time for Sarah to stop looking through the rearview mirror as she drives down the road of life. She will discover new horizons, emotional freedom, and a stronger relationship with her husband when she focuses on the broad windshield of the future. And no, it is not absolutely necessary for her to confess her prior indiscretion with her husband. Her decision to do so must be anchored in prayer with thoughtful consideration of his level of spiritual and emotional maturity to handle such truth. Otherwise, her confession could cause him to begin to distrust her and thus create a new set of problems.

Obedience and Security

When you know you have behaved in a manner consistent with godly standards, you have an inner sense of security and strength. Jesus' confidence came from knowing He obeyed God. "And He who sent Me is with Me; He has not left Me alone, for I always do the things that are pleasing to Him" (John 8:29 NASB). The apostle John echoed a similar conviction. "Dear friends, if our conscience is clear, we can come to God with bold confidence. And we will receive whatever we request because we obey him and do the things that please him" (1 John 3:21-22 NLT).

Many years ago I worked as a vice president in an entertainment conglomerate. The company was preparing to be acquired by another entity. However, I was devastated to learn that the subsidiary where I was employed would be shut down within the following year as part of corporate restructuring. I held a plumb position that came with a tastefully decorated office—and a very nice compensation package so typical of the entertainment industry. I was certainly not looking forward to a job search.

The salaries in the entertainment industry in general tended to be much higher at that time than other industries. I knew it would be difficult to find a new position with similar benefits, and so I started to become a little anxious. The first thing my husband asked me when I told him that my subsidiary would be shut down was, "Is there any sin in your life?" (Imagine!) I assured him I was current regarding confession of sin. I try to make it a habit to keep the door of repentance swinging so that my channel to God stays clear. He then assured me that we could relax and believe God for His provision.

With confidence in God's promise to multiply the seeds we had planted not only in our church, but also in the lives of others, and with confidence that we had walked in obedience and integrity with our finances, I released all anxiety—that is, until about 30 days before the designated shutdown date. I had not received a single job offer—primarily due to the fact that I had only advised a few acquaintances of my plight and had not sent out any résumés. One Saturday Darnell and I were riding in the car and I exclaimed in frustration, "Lord, if You let me down, I'm going to tell everybody." Imagine, threatening to ruin God's reputation. Appalled at my statement, Darnell replied, "God, that is her side of the car. Please don't strike me dead." A few weeks later, a Fortune 500 company, through an executive recruiter, offered me a high-level position at a 20 percent raise! The job was created and the responsibilities defined *after* I had been on board several weeks with very little to do. God had done it again! I do not believe I could have had the confidence to believe for such a miracle if I had had to wrestle with a guilty conscience for living in disobedience.

We need to make every effort to line our lives up with God's requirements. When we do so, it has a big impact on our sense of security. "The fruit of righteousness will be peace; the effect of righteousness will be quietness and confidence forever" (Isaiah 32:17).

CONFIDENCE CHALLENGE

⊘· Do you have an *unconfessed* sin that is keeping you from walking in total confidence? Repent now and accept God's forgiveness.

⊘· Are you still repenting over a sin you committed long ago? Can you rest now that you know God doesn't even remember it?

Perfectionism

*Have you lost your senses? After starting your
Christian lives in the Spirit, why are you now trying
to become perfect by your own human effort?*

GALATIANS 3:3 NLT

O YOU BEAT YOURSELF UP when, despite your best efforts, you fall short of your expectations? Do you feel that what you accomplish is never really good enough? Are you slow to make a decision or turn in a project because you must make sure it is just right? Is your quest to be blameless really an attempt to protect yourself from criticism and disapproval? Are you always trying to improve upon a physical aspect of yourself people already admire? If you answered yes to any of the above, here is my last question: Are you ready to leave the prison of perfectionism?

Perfectionism is a mind-set of self-defeating thoughts and behaviors aimed at reaching unrealistic goals. Famed psychologist Dr. David Viscott explained it this way:

> A controlling adult's wish to be perfect stems from the childhood wish to be blameless. Since real growth means embracing your faults and examining your weaknesses, controlling people run the greatest risk of

becoming rigid and failing because of their insistence on always being right. They need to feel they are beyond criticism so that no one will have a good reason for withholding what they need or rejecting them. They believe they need to be perfect just to be safe, so admitting even small imperfections makes them uneasy and self-doubting. If they can be imperfect in one way, they reason, they could be imperfect in others. Since being imperfect is a fact of life, acknowledging themselves honestly is a continual threat to their self-esteem. Even slight criticisms compel them to refute others' logic and testimony. [2]

In today's society, many people believe that being a perfectionist is desirable and necessary for success. Therefore, they wear their perfectionism like a badge of honor and a source of pride. God forbid they should break free of behavior that society applauds. The real truth is that perfectionism is a major roadblock to achieving emotional security.

In this chapter I am going to challenge you to confront your perfectionist behavior in three areas: spiritual perfection, performance perfection, and physical perfection. My goal is to get you to abandon the thinking that robs you of the peace, productivity, and personal satisfaction you can experience once you accept the weaknesses, imperfections, and shortcomings inherent in being human. You will never be able to experience emotional security if you feel you must make sure everything associated with you is perfect.

Spiritual Perfection

The Pharisees were a miserable lot. This sect of the Jews sought perfection in the observance of the laws of Moses and the traditions of their elders. They were so sanctimonious that they even separated themselves from other Jews. They railed on any Jew—including Jesus—who did not comply with their strict interpretations of the law. They criticized the fact that He did not engage in ceremonial hand washing before He ate, that He healed people on the Sabbath day, and that He seemed to disregard a number of their traditions. Jesus, being the secure person that He was, refused to become a puppet of their opinions. His response to them sometimes seemed downright offensive. He called them hypocrites and told people to beware of them.

Why was Jesus so adamantly opposed to this group? Because not only did He come to usher in a covenant of grace that would fulfill and transcend the law, but He also knew how futile it was to strive for human perfection. Notwithstanding, He seemed to contradict Himself when He commanded His disciples, "But you are to be perfect, even as your Father in heaven is perfect" (Matthew 5:48 NLT). Was Jesus engaging in double-talk? Of course not. We find clarity in His mandate when we take a careful look at the meaning of the word "perfect." To be perfect is to be complete or mature. The perfection God requires is simply a heart mature in love and completely sold out to doing His will His way. Nowhere does the Bible equate sinlessness with perfection. The apostle Paul understood this fact all too well. He confessed, "I don't mean to say that I have already achieved these things or that I have already reached perfection! But I keep working toward that day when I will finally be all that Christ Jesus saved me for and wants me to be" (Philippians 3:12 NLT).

The perfection God requires is simply a heart mature in love and completely sold out to doing His will His way.

Our goal indeed should be to live free of sin. However, our Lord knew that as fallible humans we would occasionally fall short of His requirements, whether in words, thoughts, or deeds. Therefore, He put a stopgap measure in place to deal with our transgressions. "My dear children, I am writing this to you so that you will not sin. But if you do sin, there is someone to plead for you before the Father. He is Jesus Christ, the one who pleases God completely" (1 John 2:1 NLT). Jesus was the only person who walked in human flesh who could claim perfection.

Failure can be a teaching tool. God is never surprised or shocked when we fail. He is all-knowing; He knows what we will do long before we do it. Neither is He ever disappointed by our actions, because to be disappointed is to experience an unmet expectation.

In spite of our deeds, God stands ready to forgive us the moment we repent. "He has removed our rebellious acts as far away from us as the east is from the west. The LORD is like a father to his children, tender and compassionate to those who fear him. For he understands how weak we are; he knows we are only dust" (Psalm 103:12-14 NLT).

When we come to understand that failure can be a key tool in our spiritual and emotional development, we will stop our self-flogging and guilt tripping. Instead, we will embrace the convicting power of the Holy Spirit, ask and accept God's forgiveness, and move forward—much like the apostle Paul. "No, dear brothers and sisters, I am still not all I should be, but I am focusing all my energies on this one thing: Forgetting the past and looking forward to what lies ahead, I strain to reach the end of the race and receive the prize for which God, through Christ Jesus, is calling us up to heaven" (Philippians 3:13-14 NLT). There is no need to wander in the desert of condemnation when God has a promised land waiting to be inhabited. Rather than asking, "How could this happen to me?" or "Will I ever be fit for His service?" we need to ask ourselves, "What lesson can I learn from this?" The real tragedy in failing occurs when we keep going around the same mountain and making the same mistakes.

Performance Perfection

There are those who, rather than seeking to perfect their relationship with God, choose instead to gain man's accolades through impeccable performance. Meet an acquaintance whom I will call Denise. Denise is an inflexible, nitpicking pain in the neck. Everything has to be done according to her unrealistically high standards. She grew up in the proverbial fishbowl and quickly learned that, as the pastor's daughter, she was expected to be blameless in every aspect of her existence. Denise tried to avoid making mistakes at all costs lest she embarrass her father or otherwise tarnish the family's perfect image. Though she has long since become an adult and is no longer subject to the scrutiny of her father's judgmental congregation, she continues to seek perfection in everything she does. She is overly sensitive to any constructive input. She bristles at the slightest suggestion of an improvement in her cast-in-stone plans.

Denise's unending attempts to be perfect alienates others. It also sours her relationships with those who would dare to assist her in various charitable projects. Needless to say, her perfectionism keeps her in a vicious performance cycle. She establishes unrealistic standards for herself or others and labels herself (or them) a failure for not being able to meet those standards. With each new project, she starts the process all over again more determined to make it perfect this time around. Each experience only serves to further erode her sense of security. To this date, she has not learned the difference between perfectionism and the healthy pursuit of excellence. Consequently, she gets very little fulfillment out of her noble efforts to help others.

Denise needs to understand the root of her perfectionism. She must honestly answer the question: "What am I really afraid of?" Next, she must ask herself, "What is the worst that could happen if things don't turn out perfectly?" When she stops and considers the possible outcomes, she may find out that her fears don't have as strong a foundation as she thought.

Is making a mistake really such a tragedy? I have dealt with my own performance perfectionism with some success. For example, I realized that when I have demanded perfection from my staff, my real fear was that any mistakes they made would cause others to think I was personally incompetent. My department was high profile because it served the entire organization. It seemed that the staff was bent on sabotaging my image—or that's how I perceived it since the buck stopped with me. They knew I did not tolerate poor performance; therefore, they felt that each mistake brought them closer to being fired. After a series of staff mistakes, I was at my wit's end. I had documented procedures, encouraged questions, maintained an open-door policy, and had done all that I knew to ensure an efficient operation. I earnestly prayed for a breakthrough. God gave me a new mind-set and a new strategy for the situation. I called a staff meeting and set everyone free from perfection prison. I asked them to do their very best and to note ways to avoid repeating the same mistakes in the future. I even shared with them several instances in which I had made mistakes. A marvelous thing happened. Their anxiety levels dropped and morale soared. The finger-pointing virtually stopped because team solutions became more important than placing blame. In our staff meetings, we even started to find humor in some of the errors—which, by the way, decreased significantly.

Performance perfectionists must learn to enjoy the process of achieving their goals without obsessing over the end result.

It was never my intention for my pursuit of excellence to turn into the anxiety-producing perfectionism that caused me and them frustration that negatively impacted the quality of all of our lives.

My experiences have taught me that performance perfectionists must learn to enjoy the process of achieving their goals without obsessing over the end result. They must become flexible and mature enough to solicit and pay attention to honest feedback. Most importantly, perfectionists must submit all of their plans to God and believe He will work things out for good as they follow His leading. I find it interesting that Noah, an amateur guided by God, built the ark while professionals, using the best of man's wisdom, built the *Titanic*. The ark fulfilled its purpose. The *Titanic* sank.

Physical Perfection

Obesity is the number one health concern in the United States. It is interesting to note, however, that it is not always the obese who are obsessing over their physical appearance. Rather, it is primarily the people—especially women—who are already within an acceptable weight range who are striving to achieve physical perfection.

I live in Southern California, where it seems that physical beauty is worshiped more than God. Of course, the presence of the television and film industry here with its skilled makeup and makeover artists have established a beauty standard that only a few can achieve. Still, Hollywood's influence has permeated the entire country and even the world. It is no wonder insecurity reigns among the masses.

For some women, especially those who can afford it (and even some who cannot), the slightest imperfection necessitates a call to a "fix it" specialist. Beauty-enhancing surgeries abound despite the fact that many people have died or experienced serious complications trying to achieve the perfect body or face.

Some people become insecure about their best features. For example, suppose people often tell a woman that she has beautiful hair, teeth, or skin. Before long, she may start obsessing with ways to make sure that the complimented feature is always perfect. Some women have actually ruined something that was naturally beautiful by trying to perfect it.

The big question here is how far should God's children go to maximize their attractiveness? What does the Bible say about altering the unique deck of physical cards God has dealt?

Designed for Destiny

Did you know God dictated our unchangeable physical features before we even entered this world? The psalmist declared, "You made all the delicate, inner parts of my body and knit me together in my mother's womb" (Psalm 139:13 NLT). According to the prophet Isaiah, each aspect of our body was designed to fulfill His divine purpose. "And now the LORD speaks—he who formed me in my mother's womb to be his servant" (Isaiah 49:5 NLT). God deliberately shaped each of us for His service. How then can we complain that we are too short, too tall, too dark, too fair, or too anything that is unchangeable? The word "too" implies that something is beyond what is desirable or more than what should be. Such a declaration about God's creation is a rejection of His judgment. How can anything that God formed be *too* anything? What we are really saying is, "This feature does not conform to society's prescribed standard of beauty." Thus, we allow our nonconforming attributes to cause us to become insecure and rob us of our confidence. We then feel that our only solution is to change the undesirable feature. What a slap in God's face. Listen to what He has to say about our rejection of His judgment:

> *How can anything that God formed be too anything?*

> Destruction is certain for those who argue with their Creator. Does a clay pot ever argue with its maker? Does the clay dispute with the one who shapes it, saying, "Stop, you are doing it wrong!" Does the pot exclaim, "How clumsy can you be!" How terrible it

would be if a newborn baby said to its father and mother, "Why was I born? Why did you make me this way?" This is what the LORD, the Creator and Holy One of Israel, says: "Do you question what I do? Do you give me orders about the work of my hands?" (Isaiah 45:9-11 NLT).

Because we cannot perfect what God has already perfected for His purpose, our objective should be to accept the work of His hands. How do we do this? Does accepting our features mean we have to like them?

Before we explore the answers to these questions, let's distinguish between changeable and unchangeable features. Though God dictated our vertical dimension (height), our horizontal dimension (weight) has been, in large part, dictated by our diet and exercise habits. Height is unchangeable; weight can be managed even in spite of heredity factors. Examples of other unchangeable features include your eyes, nose, complexion, body build, and ethnicity, to name a few.

You will strengthen your emotional security when you make peace with every aspect of yourself. By God's grace and divine enablement, you must truly accept—not merely resign yourself to—His sovereign design. When you do so, you stop comparing yourself to others and judging yourself inferior or superior. Self-consciousness and fretting with the outward appearance disappear. You have now cleared the path for your real, inner beauty to shine through.

Correcting Distractions

If a physical attribute *detracts* from your ability to communicate or to be effective, and God gives you the means and the go-ahead to correct it, then by all means proceed.

In my early twenties I met and dated a young man who had a front tooth that was significantly larger than its mate. He was a brilliant up-and-coming junior executive with great oratory skills. Unfortunately, I could not help but focus on that tooth the entire time he was speaking. I finally mustered the courage to recommend a good dentist, who subsequently capped and brought alignment to his front teeth. His smile improved significantly. The last I heard of him, he was still climbing the corporate ladder.

What is the condition of your smile? Investing in the best smile you can afford is money well spent. Your smile can be your most effective calling card and an instant reflection of the love of God in your heart.

If filling a gap between your teeth, having a prominent mole removed, incorporating a weave into thinning hair, or correcting any other distracting feature will enhance your effectiveness, then it will be money put to good use and do wonders for your self-esteem. Don't wait for someone else to point this out to you. Just take an honest look in the mirror. Or ask an honest friend who really loves you. I ran into an elderly woman recently who had her teeth fixed. She always wore beautiful clothes, but her mouth resembled a jack-o'-lantern. I remarked how beautiful her smile was. She said that no one had ever told her she needed to have the cosmetic work done, yet I had heard several people talk about it.

> *Know that you are designed for your destiny, tailored for your tasks, and perfect for your purpose.*

Remember that the primary purpose of any physical correction should be to eliminate or minimize distractions for your message rather than trying to perfect God's design.

Abandoning physical perfectionism is not about liking yourself but about trusting God enough to accept and rejoice in His physical design. I often remind myself that God needs me to be 5′ 2″, have coarse hair, and to possess several other physical attributes in order to fulfill His purpose in my life.

It is time to experience body peace. Know that you are designed for your destiny, tailored for your tasks, and perfect for your purpose.

CONFIDENCE CHALLENGE

- Because people will connect with you better through your vulnerability and your weaknesses, learn to accept your own humanity and to become more touchable. Identify specific perfectionist behaviors in various areas of your life (spiritual, performance, physical) and make a conscious decision to put an end to them.

- Name one thing that you will work on specifically.

Pride

❦

God resists the proud,
but gives grace to the humble.

1 PETER 5:5 NKJV

RIDE, THAT INORDINATE SENSE of one's superiority, has been at the root of some of the world's greatest tragedies. It can destroy a person's life faster than a speeding bullet. The Scriptures remind us of how much God hates pride. It was because of pride that Lucifer tried to exalt himself above God and in so doing persuaded a host of angels to rebel in heaven (Isaiah 14). Pride made its mark on the earth. It was pride that caused Ahithophel to commit suicide because Absalom did not take his advice (2 Samuel 17:23). Pride caused Haman to plot the death of Mordecai and all the Jews because Mordecai would not bow to him (Esther 3:5). God brought disaster on the prosperous coastal city of Tyre to destroy their pride and to "show his contempt for all human greatness" (Isaiah 23:8 NLT). Proud people never come to a good end.

Benjamin Franklin said, "There is perhaps not one of our natural passions so hard to subdue as pride. Beat it down, stifle it, mortify it as much as one pleases, it is still alive. Even if I could conceive that I had completely overcome it, I should probably be proud of my humility."

Pride loves the spotlight and the glory of getting the credit. A coworker told me a story of two ducks and a frog who lived happily together in a farm pond. The best of friends, the three would amuse themselves and play together in their water hole.

> *If the self-exalted one refuses to humble himself, he leaves God with no other choice than to do it for him.*

When the hot summer days came, however, the pond began to dry up, and soon it was evident they would have to move. This was no problem for the ducks, who could easily fly to another pond. But the frog was stuck. After some thought, he came up with a brilliant plan. He suggested that the ducks put a stick in their bills so that he could hang tightly on to it with his mouth as they flew to another pond a few miles away. The plan worked well—so well, in fact, that as they were flying along several people looked up and applauded their ingenuity. With each accolade, the frog grew in pride. Just as they were about to reach their destination, a farmer looked up in admiration and exclaimed, "Well, isn't that a clever idea! I wonder who thought of it?" Eager to claim credit, the frog yelled, "I did!"—and plunged to his death. "Pride goes before destruction, a haughty spirit before a fall" (Proverbs 16:18).

Pride Prevents Divine Intimacy

Because God resists the proud, a person who walks in pride cannot experience a close, intimate, and confidence-producing relationship with Him. Their pride blinds them to their insignificance when compared to Almighty God. Their estimation of themselves is as ridiculous as the flea who told the elephant, "Brace yourself. I'm about to jump off!"

God will not tolerate pride from anyone. If the self-exalted one refuses to humble himself, he leaves God with no other choice than to do it for him. Ask King Nebuchadnezzar. His pride got the best of him one day when he was taking a stroll on the roof of his palace. "As he looked out across the city, he said, 'Just look at this great city of Babylon! I, by my own mighty power, have built this beautiful city as my royal residence and as an expression of my royal splendor'" (Daniel 4:30 NLT). Imagine taking credit for all that God had given him. A year earlier Daniel had told the king through the interpretation of his dream that he should

A man wrapped in himself makes a pretty small package.

change his ways. He had ignored Daniel's warning. Now, enough was enough. God interrupted his proud moment. "While he was still speaking these words, a voice called down from heaven, 'O King Nebuchadnezzar, this message is for you! You are no longer ruler of this kingdom'" (Daniel 4:31 NLT). In the words of billionaire entrepreneur Donald Trump: "You're fired!" God banished Nebuchadnezzar to the fields for seven years. He had to eat grass like a cow. He no longer had the privileges of personal grooming. His hair grew as long as eagles' feathers, and his nails were like birds' claws. He lost his sanity. His pride had brought him low. He had become too self-absorbed. Someone once said, "A man wrapped in himself makes a pretty small package."

God took Nebuchadnezzar so far down that, after seven years, the only direction he could look was up. He had finally learned that God rules in the affairs of men and gives kingdoms to whomever He wishes. Nebuchadnezzar's pride had cost him everything. Now, he was ready to walk in humility. When he humbled himself, God had mercy on him and gave him back his sanity and his reign. He came from the fields declaring God's sovereignty over kings and kingdoms. "Now I, Nebuchadnezzar, praise and glorify and honor the King of heaven. All his acts are just and true, and he is able to humble those who are proud" (Daniel 4:37 NLT).

The Self-Confidence Trap

Pride promotes self-reliance. It tells us we can indeed do things on our own. In our attempt to walk in self-confidence, we slam the door in God's face and shut out the work of the Holy Spirit, our helper.

The apostle Paul could boast of being educated, sophisticated, and consecrated, yet he humbly declared, "By the grace of God I am what I am: and his grace which was bestowed upon me was not in vain; but I laboured more abundantly than they all: yet not I, but the grace of God which was with me" (1 Corinthians 15:10 KJV).

For many years I was a staunch advocate of self-confidence. I embraced the teachings of secular motivational speakers who convinced me that if I believed in *myself*, the sky was the limit in terms of what I could accomplish. However, having faced several professional and personal situations that required greater skills, knowledge, and mental fortitude than I possessed, I began to realize that my self-confidence was woefully inadequate. Smarts can only take you so far. I needed to rely on something or someone bigger and better equipped.

As explained in a previous chapter, the core meaning of the word "confidence" is "with faith." Self-confidence stresses faith or trust in one's powers, abilities, or capacities. General George S. Patton once asserted, "The most vital quality a soldier can possess is self-confidence." Of course I understand the general's attempt to motivate the troops with this worldly advice. However, it was just that—worldly advice. The most *detrimental* quality we can have is self-confidence. Jesus explained why. "I am the vine; you are the branches. If a man remains in me and

I in him, he will bear much fruit; apart from me you can do nothing" (John 15:5).

Since we can do nothing apart from God, it seems that the focus of our faith or confidence should be on Him and not ourselves.

When Confidence Fails

Self-confidence causes us to act independently of God. Further, when a self-confident person fails relying on his own strength, he is often devastated by the painful realization of his inadequacy. His pride won't let him accept full responsibility for the failure, so he blames others or situations over which he claims he has no control. His self-confidence has now become a stumbling block to his sense of peace and security.

On the other hand, when the plans of a person walking in Supreme confidence go awry, he is wise enough to subordinate his desires to the sovereign will of God. He quickly reminds himself that "many are the plans in a man's heart, but it is the LORD's purpose that prevails" (Proverbs 19:21). He is convinced that God has a higher purpose for his life and that no man can thwart it. Therefore, he has no need to wallow on the ground of disappointment.

Confidence in Man

While some people struggle with pride and self-confidence, there are some who put their faith in the strength of others. For example, King Asa of Judah had a perfect heart toward God. Unlike his predecessors, he rejected the idols of his day and made every attempt to walk uprightly before God. Notwithstanding, when an enemy nation came against him, he panicked. He purchased a military alliance with another king with funds he took from the house of God. Upon hearing the news of Asa's coalition with another strong, well-equipped army, his enemy retreated. Mission accomplished. Asa had figured out the solution. His plan had worked—or so it seemed.

God sent the prophet Hanani to reprimand Asa for his faithless act: "Because you have relied on the king of Syria, and have not relied on the LORD your God, therefore the army of the king of Syria has escaped from your hand. Were the Ethiopians and the Lubim not a huge army with very many chariots and horsemen? Yet, because you relied on the LORD, He delivered them into your hand" (2 Chronicles 16:7-8 NKJV).

Despite his strong moral convictions, Asa did what we have all been guilty of doing at some point in our lives—he acted independently of God. He simply did what made sense and relied on the arm of flesh. This is often the plight of those who are highly logical and intelligent. Their confidence is in their ability to *figure out* a solution to their dilemmas. A pattern of doing only what makes sense can be a major roadblock to developing emotional security. If you are ever going to walk in Supreme confidence, you must shift your thinking gear from "natural" to "spiritual."

Asa frustrated God's grace by not relying on Him. Imagine God sitting on His throne and declaring, "I had a solution that would have been far superior to yours. I had a miracle waiting that would have blown your mind. But your faith was limited to what you could rationalize."

Hanani continued his rebuke to Asa. "For the eyes of the LORD run to and fro throughout the whole earth, to show Himself strong on behalf of those whose heart is loyal to Him. In this you have done foolishly; therefore from now on you shall have wars" (2 Chronicles 16:9).

Asa relied on the flesh rather than on the Lord. Later in his life, when he developed a life-threatening disease in his feet, he "did not seek help from the LORD, but only from the physicians" (2 Chronicles 16:12). They could not help him, and so he died. Here was a righteous man who chose to live by facts rather than faith.

Beware of Your Strong Suit

Sometimes we become so secure because of our track record in a certain area that we assume we will always be victorious. Pastor Frank Wilson tells the story of a church that was so impressed with a certain deacon's years of humble service that they voted to award him a "badge of humility." They were chagrined the next Sunday when he came to church sporting it on the lapel of his suit. The pastor graciously took it away from him.

> *We are most likely to fall, most apt to be blindsided, and most apt to be caught off guard when we are most confident of our own strength.*

We are most likely to fall, most apt to be blindsided, and most apt to be caught off guard when we are most confident of our own strength. Paul warns, "If you think you are standing firm, be careful that you don't fall!" (1 Corinthians 10:12).

It just doesn't pay to brag or even to be subtly proud of our strengths. I have always asserted that I can keep my cool in any emotionally charged situation. I have practiced for years staying calm and responding in an even tone. During a recent conversation with a friend, I reiterated that this was indeed a strong suit that has worked for me for years. Within a few days of our discussion, I encountered a man who pushed a button I didn't even know I had. I found myself yelling at him at the top of my voice. I had never done that before or since. I will never be able to boast of this strength again. Since then, I have ceased claiming any personal strong suits. I've decided to follow Paul's example. "That is why, for Christ's sake, I delight in weaknesses...in difficulties. For when I am weak, then I am strong" (2 Corinthians 12:10). By no means am I suggesting that we should go around talking about how weak we are. I am cautioning that we must stay *mindful* that our security in any situation is based in God and not on our own strength.

CONFIDENCE CHALLENGE

- Read the fourth chapter of the book of Daniel and see how King Nebuchadnezzar could have avoided his fall from grace.

- Are you challenged by a proud spirit? Specifically, what is the object of your pride (a particular accomplishment, physical attractiveness, a talent)?

- It is time to let the Holy Spirit empower you to conquer this insidious emotional enemy.

PART III

SEVEN STRATEGIES FOR CONQUERING THE GIANT OF INSECURITY

Strat·e·gy: a plan of action intended
to accomplish a specific goal

STRATEGY 1

Rest on God's Word

Who is this uncircumcised Philistine
that he should defy the armies of the living God?

1 SAMUEL 17:26

ET'S FACE IT. Insecurity makes us uneasy and apprehensive. Yet God's desire for His children is that they would not be anxious for anything. He wants us to rest on His Word. Entering that rest is the challenge every problem presents to us today, and it was the challenge that faced the Israelites who found themselves confronted with the supersized human called Goliath.

Fourteen generations before the battle with Goliath, God gave Abraham His word about how He would take care of him. He promised, "I will bless those who bless you, and whoever curses you I will curse" (Genesis 12:3). Later, when He extended this and a host of other promises to Abraham's descendents, He inserted a key provision:

> This is my covenant with you and your descendants
> after you, the covenant you are to keep: Every male
> among you shall be circumcised. You are to undergo

circumcision, and it will be the sign of the covenant between me and you (Genesis 17:10-11).

Abraham believed God's promises. So did David. David knew his circumcision made him an heir to the covenant. Thus, he could not help becoming righteously indignant when he came to the scene of the battle to bring food supplies and saw all of those circumcised Israelites running from the giant. Apparently no one remembered that the Jews had a covenant with God. He felt compelled to ask, "Who is this *uncircumcised* Philistine that he should defy the armies of the living God?" (1 Samuel 17:26, emphasis added).

David was in essence asking, "How could this man, who has no covenant with God, even think about conquering us?" Sadly, in fleeing from the giant, the Israelites proved that they had no confidence in that covenant. Can you relate to their action? How strong is your faith in God's promise to bless, protect, and prosper those who are in right standing with Him? If we continue to run from the giants in our lives, we will never see the power of God manifested.

Goliath had taunted the Israelites for 40 days before David came on the scene. Had any of the soldiers, including King Saul their leader, believed the covenant, they could have taken care of Goliath themselves.

When you believe God's promises, you do not have to tolerate any giant in your life. We are heirs to the same covenant that God gave to Abraham. "If you belong to Christ, then you are Abraham's seed, and heirs according to the promise" (Galatians 3:29). How long have you tolerated the giant of insecurity? Do you believe that "God is able to make *all* grace abound to you, so that in *all* things at *all* times, having *all* that you need, you will abound in *every* good work" (2 Corinthians 9:8, emphasis added)? Or have you chosen to let insecurity reign in your life and keep you from pursuing your goals or from having meaningful, trusting relationships? Left unchecked, insecurity will become a stronghold that will influence everything you do.

Learning and Resting

Too many of God's children think the Bible is not really for today, that many of its promises are now antiquated. They are sadly mistaken. David rested on a promise of protection that was 14 generations old, and it is still good now. Unlike supermarket fare, the Word of God endures forever; there are no expiration dates on His promises. We must be diligent to hide them in our heart. For every project I embark on, I print out and memorize or refer often to passages from the Bible that remind me that apart from God I can do nothing and that He is faithful to complete whatever work He starts in me. For me, such Scriptures take the focus, the weight, and the responsibility from me and put them on Him.

It is not enough, however, to simply memorize Scripture. There is a difference between *learning* the Word and *resting* on it. Rest implies that we have ceased our negative thoughts and speculations. Our minds have stopped the doubting, stopped rehearsing what-if scenarios, and stopped being influenced by present realities. In appendix B is a listing of insecurity-banishing Scriptures that are sure to address any insecurity that has plagued your life. As you meditate on them, you will soon realize that there is no insecurity that is outside of God's ability to heal. Nothing is too hard for Him. He said so. "I am the LORD, the God of all mankind. Is anything too hard for me?" (Jeremiah 32:27).

The story of David and Goliath is representative of many of the battles we face on a regular basis: good over evil; God's power over man's strength, and faith over fear. Whatever the situation, when the dust settles we are left with one abiding truth: We can rest on God's Word. "Now we who have believed enter that rest, just as God has said" (Hebrews 4:3).

CONFIDENCE CHALLENGE

⊘· Write out and memorize the following personalized paraphrased version of 2 Corinthians 9:8, noting the emphasized words.

> God is able to make **all** grace abound toward me, so that I, in **all** things at **all** times, having **all** that I need, will abound in **every** good work.

⊘· Make a conscious decision to rest on these words in the coming weeks. Share them with a friend.

Refuse to Be Deterred

You are not able to go out
against this Philistine and fight him; you are only a boy,
and he has been a fighting man from his youth.

1 SAMUEL 17:33

REST ASSURED THAT THERE will always be people who will try to prevent or discourage you from killing your giant of insecurity or any other giant in your life. Their resistance could be due to the fact that "misery loves company," or they are projecting their lack of faith onto you, or they have any other reasons to keep you locked in your cell of inadequacy. Whatever the intention, you may find that you have to stand alone in your quest. Don't wait for the support of a cheerleading squad before you get started.

David met with discouragement as soon as he came to the battlefield and asked why everyone was running from Goliath. We read in the chapter on the "Eliab Syndrome" that Eliab, David's oldest brother, accused him of being a conceited show-off simply for being on the scene. "'Now what have I done?' said David. 'Can't I even speak?' *He then turned away to someone else* and brought up the same matter" (1 Samuel 17:29, emphasis added). David's response represents a key strategy in dealing with discouragers. It reminds me of my elders in the South. When they wanted to let someone know they were ignoring his comments, they would say, "I'm not studin' you!" To study was to give something careful thought and consideration. When David turned from Eliab to speak to the other men, he was in essence saying to him, "I'm not studin' you! I'm going to ignore you and focus on someone else." We can easily fall into the trap of giving too much thought and consideration to the discourager.

To think we are inadequate for a task is to engage in self-centeredness.

There was more discouragement David had to face. Even King Saul, also a fellow heir to the Abrahamic covenant, cautioned him against confronting Goliath. "David said to Saul, 'Let no one lose heart on account of this Philistine; your servant will go and fight him.' Saul replied, 'You are not able to go out against this Philistine and fight him; you are only a boy, and he has been a fighting man from his youth'" (1 Samuel 17:32-33).

David, however, was not concerned about how much experience Goliath had because David knew that God was all-powerful. How tragic it is when we limit our faith to only what we can see. To think we are inadequate for a task is to engage in self-centeredness. We begin to focus on what we perceive our own capabilities to be apart from God. This independent mindset shuts Him out of the equation and ignores the fact that He has declared that His strength is made perfect in weakness. God doesn't call the qualified; He qualifies the called.

Discouraging Christians

If you are a Christian, there is a good chance that some of your resistance will come from those who are heirs to the same promises you claim. Like Eliab, whose name meant "God is my father," God's children can be resentful or envious of your desire to conquer your giant. You must make an independent decision to persevere until you have the victory.

Let's say you are insecure about speaking in public, not only because of your noticeably Southern accent, but also because you need to shed more than a few pounds. Notwithstanding, you have a great command of English and the church needs volunteers in this area of ministry for the weekly announcements. Though you have rationalized for the past two months that waiting until next year to volunteer would give you time to take a class to get rid of your accent, as well as time to complete a weight loss program, you press past your self-imposed arguments and decide to do it now. However, you make the mistake of telling your shy, plump friend Betty. The two of you have

> *You cannot afford to allow another person's input, which emanates from their insecurity, to reinforce your own.*

enjoyed sitting in the back of the church together each Sunday and passing an occasional note to each other. Why, a few times you snickered at a mistake the announcement clerk made in her pronunciation of certain words. To your disappointment, Betty discourages you from participating. "Girl, they are going to call you 'country' if you get up there with that Southern drawl. And have you noticed how thin those clerks are? It must be an unwritten requirement. I'll bet you'll be buying some fancier clothes too. You see how sophisticated they all dress—just because they have to sit on the platform when it's their turn to make announcements. Humph!"

How would you reply to Betty's comments? Would you say, "Get thee behind me, Satan. I have a giant to kill"? Well, not really. Even though you understand what is motivating her comments, you must still respond in love. "Betty, I'm aware of all of the *facts*. The *truth*, however, is that I feel that God wants me to serve in this capacity, so I'm going for it. He can handle the rest."

You cannot afford to allow another person's input, which emanates from their insecurity, to reinforce your own. You have to handle such discouragers the same way you would handle any toxic substance: Eliminate or limit your exposure to it. When you must come into contact with it, protect yourself with the proper attire—that is, the whole armor of God (see Ephesians 6:11-18).

Nehemiah's enemies tried every trick in the book to deter him from rebuilding the wall of the city of Jerusalem, which lay in ruins. Notice how he handled their opposition.

> Sanballat and Geshem sent me this message: "Come, let us meet together in one of the villages on the plain of Ono." But they were scheming to harm me; so I sent messengers to them with this reply: "I am carrying on a great project and cannot go down. Why should the work stop while I leave it and go down to you?" Four times they sent me the same message, and each time I gave them the same answer (Nehemiah 6:2-4).

Nehemiah remained steadfast despite their efforts. Sometimes you have to repeat yourself endlessly when you really mean business about slaying your giant. You must be willing to take the put-downs, the envy, the distractions, the discouraging words, and all other opposition.

CONFIDENCE CHALLENGE

◈· Who has deterred you from slaying your giant?

◈· What will you do about it? When?

Remember Past Victories

*The LORD who delivered me from
the paw of the lion and the paw of the bear
will deliver me from the hand of this Philistine.*

1 SAMUEL 17:37

W HEN DAVID SAW that King Saul was bent on discouraging him from confronting Goliath, he decided that he'd better give him a short testimony.

> David said to Saul, "Your servant has been keeping his father's sheep. When a lion or a bear came and carried off a sheep from the flock, I went after it, struck it and rescued the sheep from its mouth. When it turned on me, I seized it by its hair, struck it and killed it. Your servant has killed both the lion and the bear; this uncircumcised Philistine will be like one of them, because he has defied the armies of the living God" (1 Samuel 17:34-36).

The ability to recall the past is one of the most powerful functions of the brain. It can be both a blessing and curse, depending on what you choose to recall. Remembering brings the emotions of the past into the "now" whether the event was positive or negative. Remembering old hurts, offenses,

When you recall positive experiences, you rekindle the courage, the joy, and the sense of accomplishment associated with the victory.

disappointments, or failures will cause all of the emotions associated with them to rush to your mind to wreak emotional havoc once again. Conversely, when you recall positive experiences, you rekindle the courage, the joy, and the sense of accomplishment associated with the victory. You can never underestimate the power of an experience to reinspire faith.

From the parting of the Red Sea to the fall of Jericho, the Israelites had numerous miracles and mind-blowing feats God had performed on their behalf. God had cautioned them about forgetting His mighty acts. "Remember well what the LORD your God did to Pharaoh and to all Egypt. You saw with your own eyes the great trials, the miraculous signs and wonders, the mighty hand and outstretched arm, with which the LORD your God brought you out. The LORD your God will do the same to all the peoples you now fear" (Deuteronomy 7:18-19).

Several years ago when I negotiated an unprecedented financing commitment for the construction of a church sanctuary, I remember feeling inadequate from time to time as I met with highly sophisticated bankers. Some of the deal terms were foreign to me, and I was concerned that my lack of familiarity would prove detrimental to the church. However, my anxiety was short-lived as I gained confidence each time I would recall that more than 14 years earlier, I had taken a job in an industry in which I had absolutely no experience. God had shown Himself strong and had allowed me to develop a reputation for being a great negotiator as well as being able to project future expenses with a high degree of accuracy. Because I was so unfamiliar with the complicated operations, I knew beyond a shadow of a doubt that God had His angels working overtime on my behalf. It was a very humbling experience. It was then that I learned to just show up as prepared as I could be, but to expect the real answers, the brilliant stuff, to come from God.

If you have allowed Satan to give you "experience amnesia" and have forgotten those times of divine intervention in your life, why not recall someone else's testimony? Faith can come from more than one direction. Recall the good things God has done for your friends, acquaintances, coworkers, and even people you have heard about on the news. Miracles are exciting no matter who the recipient is. If He did it then, He can do it again.

Finally, do a study on the miracles in the Bible. Whenever I am feeling doubtful or unsure of my ability to overcome an obstacle, I read the story of David and Goliath. In fact, this section of this book was born out of those times.

CONFIDENCE CHALLENGE

⊘· Recall a time or incident in which God brought you out of a difficult situation. Do you believe that God is the same yesterday, today, and forever?

Reject Carnal Weapons

*For the weapons of our warfare
are not carnal but mighty in God
for pulling down strongholds.*

2 CORINTHIANS 10:4 NKJV

M Y NIECE DANA IS A POLISHED, positive, personable, professional, and confident young woman. Whatever job she lands, God immediately gives her favor with those in authority. She is regularly featured in the company's newsletter for outstanding performance as she is promoted from one department to another. Unfortunately, this also makes her the object of envy for some of her coworkers, who fear that her presence threatens their future promotions. She has become a master at responding with grace to their antagonism. She cheerily greets offenders and offers to help them in any way possible. She refuses to engage in a carnal response to other people's insecurity.

Now, lest I err in assuming your understanding of spiritual jargon, let me explain that a "carnal weapon" is any response or solution that emanates from your human nature or propensities of the flesh. It is in direct opposition to a godly or spiritually inspired alternative. Carnality is the world's way of dealing with problematic issues.

King Saul, not understanding that David was not planning to have a sword fight with Goliath, offered David his armor.

> Then Saul dressed David in his own tunic. He put a coat of armor on him and a bronze helmet on his head. David fastened on his sword over the tunic and tried walking around, because he was not used to them. "I cannot go in these," he said to Saul, "because I am not used to them." So he took them off (1 Samuel 17:38-39).

David had not "proven" the heavy armor, but he had "proven" the power of Almighty God. There was no question as to which source of power and protection he was planning to use.

A "carnal weapon" is any response or solution that emanates from your human nature or propensities of the flesh.

What weapons or methods are you "used to" in dealing with your giant? If you are going to succeed in conquering the giant of insecurity in your life, you must "put off" worldly methods of dealing with it. Perfectionism, workaholism, designer clothes, a big house, a fancy car, plastic surgery, or well-connected acquaintances will not cure insecurity. The essence of insecurity is to feel "unsure, uncertain, or inadequate." You can only be certain when you connect to the One who has no deficiency.

Truth: The Ultimate Weapon

Notice that David had no qualms about admitting his inability to use King Saul's weapons. Most insecure people have a problem with being authentic. They wear a facade of confidence until it becomes a permanent mask.

Secure living requires an honest assessment and acceptance of your personal strengths and weaknesses. If you have made some bad decisions that have gotten you to where you are today, so be it. Don't act like typical victims who refuse to take responsibility for their lives. They would rather blame others for their failures and weaknesses. They may have indeed suffered a genuine inequity or loss at someone's hands. However, like a broken clock, they got stuck in the experience.

Victims have an income statement outlook on life versus a balance sheet view. An income statement is a report of all of the revenues and expenses of an entity for a period of time in the past, such as a month, a quarter, or a year. Everything reported on an income statement represents the past. No subsequent transactions can change that history. What was earned was earned; what was spent was spent.

Now the balance sheet, on the other hand, reports the assets and liabilities of an entity as of a specific point in time. As a CPA, I have always been intrigued by the fact that a balance sheet can change the very next day. When you develop a balance sheet mind-set, you understand your situation can change without regard to the reality of your past. You courageously face your liabilities while remaining aware of the fact that you do indeed have some assets. To become emotionally secure, you must have a balanced assessment of what you bring to the table and what your shortcomings are. A proud person, or one who is *pretending* to be secure, focuses only on his assets and buries his head in the sand when it comes to acknowledging his weaknesses. At the other extreme, the insecure person is so focused on his liabilities or shortcomings that he has not developed an appreciation for the attributes or qualities he possesses.

> *When you think that you only have assets, the liability that you ignore will ultimately weaken or limit the productivity of your assets.*

Honestly assessing your strengths and weaknesses is a key step to developing emotional security. Your admitted liability and weakness can be your greatest strength. When you think that you only have assets, the liability that you ignore will ultimately weaken or limit the productivity of your assets.

I have shared below my own personal assessment. In the Confidence Challenge at the end of the chapter, you will have the opportunity to do the same.

STRENGTHS/WEAKNESSES ASSESSMENT

Strengths:

> Sincere commitment to God
> Courageous in expressing boundaries
> Good organizer
> Practice integrity in all arenas of life
> Strive for excellence in all endeavors
> Comfortable at all social levels
> Formally educated
> Not a respecter of persons
> Good motivator
> Skilled at conflict management

Weaknesses:

> Impatient with the shortcomings of others
> Often speak too quickly
> Sometimes too direct
> Judge others by their productivity
> Give unsolicited self-improvement advice
> Prone to putting work before relationship

You must acknowledge what you bring to the table while also understanding how your weaknesses impact your daily interactions. This is the truth that will make you free.

David knew he could not match the physical strength of Goliath. He also knew he did not have to. "David said to the Philistine, 'You come against me with sword and spear and javelin, but I come against you in the name of the Lord Almighty, the God of the armies of Israel, whom you have defied'" (1 Samuel 17:45).

David had an intimate relationship with his Father. He knew that the mere name of God is a strong tower where the righteous run to for safety (Proverbs 18:10). No matter what giant he faced, as a "covenant holder" the battle belonged to the Lord. He was secure in that truth.

CONFIDENCE CHALLENGE

⊕· Using the format demonstrated above, make a list of your strengths and a list of your weaknesses. Solicit feedback from a trusted friend to see how truthful you have been.

Strengths:

_____

_____

_____

_____

_____

Weaknesses:

_____

_____

_____

_____

_____

Resist Intimidation

*"Come here," he said, "and I'll give
your flesh to the birds of the air
and the beasts of the field!"*

1 SAMUEL 17:44

GOLIATH TOWERED OVER DAVID as he made his threats.
Although David had to look up at him when he
responded, spiritually he was looking down upon him. He
looked at the giant through the eyes of his omnipotent God,
who sits high, looks low, and conquers all. It was God Himself
who asked the prophet Jeremiah, "Behold, I am the LORD, the
God of all flesh: is there any thing too hard for me?" (Jeremiah
32:27 KJV).

David didn't shrink back when Goliath threatened to feed
him to the birds. He wasn't intimidated. To intimidate is to
instill fear. Did you notice that the word *timid* is in the middle
of the word in*timid*ate? Satan wants the giant in our lives to
instill fear in our hearts so that it can continue to subdue us and
to keep us from going forward.

David believed God. "You come against me with sword and
spear and javelin, but I come against you in the name of the
LORD Almighty, the God of the armies of Israel, whom you have
defied" (1 Samuel 17:45).

Internal Intimidation

When battling the giant of insecurity, intimidation is most likely to come from your own erroneous assessment of your value or abilities. You can literally *think* yourself into a state of apprehension, fearfulness, and unworthiness.

Take a cartoon segment on Charlie Brown and Linus. They are having lunch at school and Charlie Brown confides to Linus that he doesn't feel good enough to approach a certain young lady. He laments, "I can't talk to that little red-haired girl because she's something and I'm nothing. Now, if I were something and she were nothing, I could talk to her, or if she were something and I were something, then I could talk to her, or if she were nothing and I were nothing, I also could talk to her...But she's something and I'm nothing, so I can't talk to her." Linus, having listened intently to his confession of his insecurity, responds, "For a nothing, Charlie Brown, you're really something." Charlie Brown had allowed the redhead's beauty to intimidate him and force him to the sidelines.

I cannot remember a time in my adult life when I have been too fearful to approach someone others have deemed important or intimidating. I refuse to believe that anybody is inherently better than I am simply because he is more wealthy, renowned, or can claim any other distinction. I endeavor to keep a "God perspective" when interacting with everybody. To Him, we are all mere flesh made from the dust of the earth. Yes, He gives some greater responsibilities, resources, and exposure, but He doesn't play favorites. We are all the same in His eyes. As the old saying goes, "The ground is level at the foot of the cross."

Talking Back to the Giant

David wasn't going to stand for Goliath's intimidation; he knew how to talk back.

David said to the Philistine, "*This day* the LORD will hand *you* over to *me*, and I'll strike *you* down and cut off *your* head.

148

Today I will give the carcasses of the Philistine army to the birds of the air and the beasts of the earth, and the whole world will know that there is a God in Israel. All those gathered here will know that it is not by sword or spear that the LORD saves; for the battle is the LORD's, and He will give all of *you* into *our* hands" (1 Samuel 17:46-47, emphasis added). What a great retort to Goliath's threats!

Are you ready to declare to your giant that "today" is the day of its demise? Whether it is the giant of insecurity, alcoholism, an unruly tongue, or a host of other self-defeating behaviors, the giant must go. You can decide to defeat him today.

CONFIDENCE CHALLENGE

⊘· Is there a person or situation that intimidates you? What declaration from the Scriptures will you make to "talk back" to your giant? (If in doubt, consult appendix B for starters.)

STRATEGY 6

Run Toward the Giant

*As the Philistine moved closer
to attack him, David ran quickly toward
the battle line to meet him.*

1 SAMUEL 17:48

ARE YOU READY TO GRAB your sword of faith and behead the giant of insecurity? Do you want to live free of the anxiety, uneasiness, uncertainty, and fears that come from anticipating a threatening event or situation?

Your best strategy will always be to attack a giant before it has a chance to get the best of you. Eleanor Roosevelt said, "You gain strength, courage, and confidence by every experience in which you really stop to look fear in the face."

Whether real or imagined, all threats are perceived as a potential for loss. It may be the loss of recognition, loss of favor, loss of affection, or even the loss of a desired relationship. Freedom begins when we stop and make an honest confession of the loss we really fear.

Acknowledging Core Fears

Identifying and acknowledging your *real* fears is a giant step toward breaking free of insecurity. To do this, you must go through the process of peeling the "fear onion" to get to the core of your anxiety or sense of inadequacy. Depending on your history of being honest with yourself, you may have to peel back a lot more layers than expected.

> *You gain strength, courage, and confidence by every experience in which you really stop to look fear in the face.*

When I served in a key financial position for a certain corporation, I knew the company's board of directors held me in esteem as a competent professional. I took pains to maintain my image in their eyes. During a particular board meeting, one of the members presented a proposal for investment of the organization's idle funds. She stated that we could probably get a much higher return than we were realizing with our current strategy. As she continued to explain her recommendation, I felt anxiety begin to rear its ugly head. Having just begun my study on insecurity only days before, I was ready to defy and reject its intrusion in my life. Now I saw that it was not going to be easy.

The more she explained her proposal, the more Satan assaulted my mind. *Why hadn't I presented that idea? Now they're going to think that I'm not so bright after all. Why didn't she run the idea by me first before presenting it to the board, even informally?* I brought my imaginations to a screeching halt and asked myself the question: "What do I fear?" The answer was quick and painful. I feared the loss of their esteem for me. I feared that the accolades I received at each board meeting would cease. God forbid! I loved those praises. I worked many uncompensated hours to be excellent—and, yes, to be recognized for being so. Now here was someone threatening my position on the pedestal. And to boot, the presenter did not even have a financial background.

Like Saul when he felt threatened with the loss of his kingdom to David, I felt anger toward this woman. However, unlike Saul, I was not going to allow insecurity to run amok in my life. I had learned from his mistake. I took a deep breath and silently recited 2 Corinthians 10:5: "Casting down imaginations, and every high thing that exalteth itself against the knowledge of God, and bringing into captivity every thought to the obedience of Christ" (KJV). My thoughts were running wild. I quickly reined them in. I knew that acknowledging my real fear would put me on the fast track to freedom. *So what that she presented a good plan to maximize our return on idle cash?* I mused. How in the world could that impact the quality of my life? Unless, of course, my life was wrapped up in trying to be the "Wonder Woman" who always has the answer to every problem.

By suggesting to me that a loss of some kind was imminent, Satan had already planted the seed of insecurity. However, having acknowledged my core fear, I quickly derailed his plan. This is the strategy we must use on thoughts of insecurity; we must attack them at a premature stage. The very nature of an attack implies proactive, aggressive action.

David did not stand there and wait for the approaching giant to subdue him. "As the Philistine moved closer to attack him, David ran quickly toward the battle line to meet him. Reaching into his bag and taking out a stone, he slung it and struck the Philistine on the forehead. The stone sank into his forehead, and he fell facedown on the ground" (1 Samuel 17:48-49). No more dialogue. The giant had to die.

Once we have decided we will conquer our insecurity, we no longer need to pay lip service to what we should do about it. We take action. *The Oprah Winfrey Show* featured a woman who decided to conquer her insecurity about her weight. She wore a size 16 dress, and while not morbidly obese, she was tired of her extreme self-consciousness. She decided that she would don a bikini and to go from house to house in her neighborhood informing the neighbors that she was overcoming her discomfort with the appearance of her body. She allowed Oprah's cameras to capture the entire experience for millions of people to watch. I don't think I could have pulled it off, but it worked for her.

Thankfully the battle we fight with the giant of insecurity is not one we fight alone. God wants to fight it for us. As Hanani told King Asa, "The eyes of the LORD range throughout the earth to strengthen those whose hearts are fully committed to him" (2 Chronicles 16:9). All that He wants from us is a commitment.

Again, the victory begins when we start to get real about what we fear and the loss that we dread.

Peeling the Onion

Answering the right questions can be like using a surgeon's scalpel in getting to the root of your fears. The exercise below will prepare you for your showdown with the giant of insecurity. Answer each question honestly. In Psalm 51:6, David declares, "You desire honesty from the heart, so you can teach me to be wise in my inmost being" (NLT). Do not lie to yourself. It's time to be honest. It is time to slay the giant of insecurity.

To help you get started, I will share the responses of one woman who will remain anonymous. At the end of the chapter, I'm going to challenge you to complete the same exercise.

Questions and Responses

1. *What situation or setting causes you to feel insecure?* I feel insecure when my friend comes over to my house dressed in sexy or seductive attire and my husband is home.

2. *What do you really fear?* I fear he will be attracted to her or become dissatisfied with me and ultimately leave me. Therefore, I fear rejection and abandonment.

3. *Is there a rational basis for this fear?* Yes. I have yet to achieve my desired weight goal. I know he would

prefer me to be slimmer despite the fact that he loves me and shows it. In addition, my friend lacks wisdom and discretion in how she interacts with him. She is a bit too familiar and crosses my comfort zone in how she responds to him.

4. *How does this insecurity cause you to behave?* I find I am overly critical of her in other areas. I also do not allow myself to get too close to her emotionally. Consequently, I limit the amount of time I spend with her, even though I enjoy her company away from my husband.

5. *Is this a godly response? If not, what behavior do you think God would consider appropriate?* Being critical of her is not a godly response. However, limiting her involvement in our lives would be wise in light of her apparent lack of wisdom. Setting clear boundaries with her and expressing my concern about specific indiscretions would be the spiritually mature thing to do.

Even though it could be a bit difficult, this exercise can also be very cathartic and liberating. The best benefit of it is that you get to put the problem out in the open, confront it, and develop a plan for overcoming it. Dale Carnegie admonished, "Do the thing you fear to do and keep on doing it. That is the quickest and surest way ever yet discovered to conquer fear."

In the next chapter we will look at the rewards of going through this exercise of exposing and confronting real fear.

CONFIDENCE CHALLENGE

- What person or situation causes you to feel insecure?

- What loss do you really fear (i.e., loss of affection, abandonment, rejection, loss of the esteem or respect of others, loss of social status, loss of control)?

- Is there a rational basis for this fear? If so, explain.

- How does this insecurity cause you to behave?

- Is this a godly response? If not, what behavior do you think God would consider appropriate?

- What practical steps are you willing to take to resolve this problem? When will you start?

Reap the Reward

What will be done for the man
who kills this Philistine and removes
this disgrace from Israel?

1 SAMUEL 17:26

SLAYING ANY GIANT IN YOUR LIFE has its rewards. When David first came to the battlefield and saw God's people running from the uncircumcised Philistine, he immediately wanted to know what his reward would be for killing him. The men responded, "The king will give great wealth to the man who kills him. He will also give him his daughter in marriage and will exempt his father's family from taxes in Israel" (1 Samuel 17:25). I'm certain these three rewards provided a great incentive to slay the giant. But, of course, it was also part of David's destiny to do so.

In this chapter we will look at tangible and intangible rewards of slaying the giant of insecurity.

Tangible Rewards

Slaying the giant of insecurity frees you from the bonds of inadequacy that have kept you from pursuing your dreams.

Let's say your insecurity is in the area of public speaking and that there is a high-paying position available in your firm that would require you to make formal presentations on a regular basis. You know the material cold, but the thought of getting up even in front of a small group causes knots to form in your stomach. But you really could use the increase in pay. What do you do? Well, don't just sit there and squander an opportunity. Remember that confidence is rooted in knowledge. If you have the technical competence, you're halfway to your goal already. Apply for the job. Believe that God will show Himself strong and help you with your presentations. In the meantime, while you are walking by faith, join a local Toastmasters group, take a public speaking class at the local college, or buy tapes or CDs that give tips for overcoming stage fright. Run toward the giant.

I have had several employees during the course of my professional career who battled insecurity. From time to time I have selected a few to be the target of my "tough love" and demanded a much higher level of performance because I knew they had the potential. Many have come back and reported their success and have thanked me for believing in them and pushing them beyond their comfort zones. I am committed to not only slaying the giants in my life but also helping others to slay their giants.

God's children have no excuse for living with insecurity when He has promised us that we can do all things through Him who strengthens us.

> *What a marked contrast between how Israel dealt with a giant before David killed Goliath and the courage they developed after he killed him.*

Intangible Rewards

One of the most significant intangible rewards of slaying a giant is the inspiration it gives to others to slay their giants.

Nobody in King Saul's army ever killed a giant. By contrast, after David killed Goliath, four other men, including his nephew, Jonathan, killed the giants that rose up against the Israelites. I read with great satisfaction and amusement the account of Jonathan's encounter with a giant.

> In still another battle, which took place at Gath, there was a huge man with six fingers on each hand and six toes on each foot—twenty-four in all. He also was descended from Rapha. When he taunted Israel, Jonathan son of Shimeah, David's brother, killed him (2 Samuel 21:20-21).

What a marked contrast between how Israel dealt with a giant *before* David killed Goliath and the courage they developed *after* he killed him. Notice in the passage above that nobody is running away. There is also a conspicuous absence of fanfare in the relating of this event. There is no blow-by-blow account of the dialog that transpired between Jonathan and the giant as there was with David and Goliath. The Bible simply states that when the giant taunted Israel, Jonathan "killed him." David had set a new standard.

Until 1954, no one had ever run a mile in under four minutes. It was the unconquerable giant in the runners' world during that time. Most people assumed it was virtually impossible for a human being to accomplish such a feat; that is, everyone except Roger Bannister. The 25-year-old British medical student used his medical knowledge to give him as much help as possible. He also researched mechanical aspects of running and used scientific training methods. On May 6, 1954, at an Oxford University track meet, Roger completed the distance in three minutes and 59.4 seconds. He had slain the giant. Unfortunately, Roger never won an Olympic medal, for Australian John Landy broke his record within two months, proving that the four-minute mile was as much a psychological as a physical barrier.[3] Notwithstanding, Bannister had set the standard.

Mount Everest is the highest peak on earth above sea level, rising approximately 5.5 miles. A normal expedition lasts 60 to 90 days. In the first half of the twentieth century, many people had attacked the formidable mountain. It was the unconquerable giant in the world of mountain climbers. On May 29, 1953, Edmund Hillary and his Sherpa guide, Tenzing Norgay, were the first humans to reach the summit. Hillary was knighted for his feat. Since then, approximately 1000 climbers, ranging from age 16 to 60, have completed the expedition.[4]

David, Bannister, and Hillary all conquered giants of their day and inspired others to match or excel their feats.

We do ourselves and others a disservice when we run from our giants. We need to stop being afraid to tackle hard tasks. If God did it then, He can do it again.

CONFIDENCE CHALLENGE

⊘· What person do you admire for being the first to accomplish a certain feat?

⊘· Do you dream of doing something that no one else has ever done? Prayerfully consider why God continues to let you dream. Could it be that someone is waiting for you to set the standard in this area?

PART IV

SEVEN HABITS OF EMOTIONALLY SECURE PEOPLE

Hab·it: a recurring pattern of behavior
acquired through frequent repetition

HABIT 1

Embracing Individuality

*One man considers one day more sacred than another;
another man considers every day alike.
Each one should be fully convinced in his own mind.*

ROMANS 14:5

I LIKE EVERY *SINGLE* INGREDIENT in vegetable juice: tomatoes, carrots, celery, beets, parsley, lettuce, watercress, and spinach. However, I can hardly stand to drink even the smallest serving of this healthy concoction. On the other hand, if you were to offer me these same ingredients in the form of a salad, I'm likely to ask for a second serving. What makes the difference? Individuality! In the vegetable juice, all of the vegetables have been blended together and have lost their distinction. Whereas with the salad, they are all in the same bowl but have retained their individual taste. So it is with emotionally secure people. They are comfortable maintaining their uniqueness while still working in harmony with those who are different.

As we take a look at seven habits of Supremely confident people, I believe that maintaining one's individuality should be at the top of the list.

Free to Be Me

Some people are just downright scared to embrace their uniqueness. They would rather live according to the "herd instinct." All of their actions or decisions are determined by the behavior of the group. The fear of being judged or rejected for being different is too great. Not so with emotionally secure people. They feel no pressure to be a carbon copy of anyone else's style or other aspect of their being. Women are notorious for resisting individuality. When I have joined in outside activities with other women, I will invariably get a call asking what I'm planning to wear—despite the fact that the official invitation to the event or the nature of the outing itself gave clear indication of what was appropriate. "Are you wearing a dress or pants?" I know that women in general have been socialized to be groupies, but I find few things more refreshing than a woman who is relaxed and comfortable with her own choices.

My friend Diane Temple is the epitome of individuality. She is a pastor's wife who has resisted the pressure to fit into anyone's mold. She is a very generous woman, a real worshiper of God, and supportive of her husband, yet she marches to the beat of her own drum when it comes to her personal style, church involvement, shopping habits, and so forth. She does not allow anyone to put her in a "should" box. Her entire demeanor says, "I'm okay with me." I cannot help but admire that rare combination of godliness and individuality. She definitely wins the prize in my book for "Mrs. Individuality."

The apostle Paul also modeled individuality. He never tried to emulate the other disciples, who had enjoyed an up close and personal relationship with Jesus. In fact, when God arrested his heart and called him to preach to the Gentiles, he did not solicit any tips or tricks of the trade from the more experienced, hands-on disciples who had walked with Jesus on a daily basis. Consider his testimony:

Then he revealed his Son to me so that I could pro-
claim the Good News about Jesus to the Gentiles.
When all this happened to me, I did not rush out to
consult with anyone else; nor did I go up to Jerusalem
to consult with those who were apostles before I was.
No, I went away into Arabia and later returned to the
city of Damascus. It was not until three years later that
I finally went to Jerusalem for a visit with Peter and
stayed there with him for fifteen days (Galatians 1:16-
18 NLT).

Although Paul could not boast an earthly relationship with
Jesus, he did not feel he brought any less to the table—even in
light of the fact that he had also persecuted and killed many
Christians. He would not allow his negative past to cause him to
feel inadequate or unworthy of his divine assignment. Why, he
was even confident enough to
rebuke Peter for his hypocrisy in
eating and fellowshiping with the
Gentiles and then ignoring them
when the Jews came around (see
Galatians 2). Can you imagine this
Johnny-come-lately rebuking the
great pillar of the church who had
so much power that his shadow had
actually healed people? Why, you'd
have to be the king of confidence to
do that.

> *Emotionally* secure people do not insist on compliance with their rigid standards that have no basis other than tradition or their personal preferences.

Free to Be You

Emotionally secure people not
only have the courage to exercise
their uniqueness, but they also sup-
port the right of another individual to be different. My brother
Vernon is such a person. He is a fun-loving, live-and-let-live
kind of guy. Whomever he meets, he embraces them and

accepts them unconditionally—no matter how weird they appear to be. He is far from being judgmental and respects everybody's right to be different. He is a true people magnet; people seem to connect with him instantly. Within minutes of meeting him, complete strangers have been known to invite him to join them in their recreational activities, to visit their homes, or to attend some special event. The rest of us siblings marvel at the favor that surrounds him.

Emotionally secure people do not insist on compliance with their rigid standards that have no basis other than tradition or their personal preferences. They do not pass judgment on those who dress differently. They do not believe that "different" means inferior—or superior. (Just for the record, I'm not condoning bizarre outfits or wild, God-dishonoring attire. Accepting another person's individuality does not mean you accept immorality. I am promoting a mind-set of love and acceptance that transcends mere physical appearance.)

Emotionally secure people do not require others to rubber-stamp their ideas or opinions—especially as they relate to nonessential matters. I know two friends who parted ways because they had different opinions about the fairness of a verdict rendered in a high-profile murder case. Whatever happened to respecting the opinion of another? By the way, if you struggle with letting others have their opinion, a key question to ask yourself is, "Will this person's stance on this matter negatively impact my life?" If not, respect it and keep moving. If the matter has eternal consequences—and most matters do not—pray that God will bring him (or maybe you) into the light of the truth.

Accept "As Is"

Have you ever purchased an item with the understanding that you were buying it "as is"? The implied agreement is that the seller has no obligation to repair any currently noted defects or any that may be subsequently discovered. Emotionally secure people know how to appreciate someone "as is." They realize that if others "zig" where they "zag," a complete picture will be produced rather than an unsolved jigsaw puzzle.

Accepting others "as is" is sometimes a bit of a challenge for me because I tend to have quite a few social "shoulds," such as "no smacking," "no white shoes after Labor Day," "no speaking in a loud volume in public," and so forth. I often have to remind myself that even though these may be the rules of etiquette, I have to accept the fact that other people may choose not to abide by them.

Many women have scared off or missed out on good mates by insisting on molding him to their graven image. I would caution any male or female to decide if he or she can truly accept a potential mate "as is." It is almost a universal paradox that when a person knows he is accepted unconditionally, he then desires to change to show you his appreciation for such acceptance. If you are looking for perfection, stop it. It will always elude you. Decide what the *essentials* are for your relationship and then accept the fact that some traits or behaviors will never measure up to your ideal standard.

Defining Essentials

A word of caution. Be careful in listening to the advice of others in the area of what your essential need is in a romantic relationship. Understand that essentials vary according to the individual. What is tolerable or acceptable for one may not be so for another. I am very clear on one thing. Although my husband loves food and delights in coming home to a great meal, if faced with the dilemma of whether to prepare a meal or to tidy the house, I know that it is more important to him to walk into a clean, clutter-free environment. This is his essential. Now, my friend Delisa would make a big mistake if, faced with the same decision, she chose to clean the house rather than cook. For her husband, food is king.

I must reiterate that essentials may be as individual as taste buds. You may require in your spouse the behavior of showing affection, having a strong work ethic, being emotionally supportive, engaging in sports and outdoor activities, traveling, and of course, having a strong commitment to God. I don't suppose I need to caution that if the person does not demonstrate the essentials during courtship, when everyone is on his or her best behavior, then it is highly unlikely that his behavior will change significantly after he says, "I do." What you see is what you'll get.

CONFIDENCE CHALLENGE

⊜· Is there an area of your life where you are fearful of being yourself? Why not take a baby step and deliberately exercise your individuality in the next week. Further, the next time that someone expresses an opinion contrary to yours, simply nod and say, "I respect your right to differ." Resist the urge to persuade them to agree with you.

Employing Teamwork

*One standing alone can be attacked
and defeated, but two can stand back-to-back
and conquer; three is even better,
for a triple-braided cord is not easily broken.*

ECCLESIASTES 4:12 TLB

THE LONE RANGER, SUPERWOMAN, Rambo, and every other "solo phenomenon" are no longer viewed as the solution to an insurmountable problem. Teamwork is in. Rock climber Nick Sagar, having triumphed over The Crew, one of the most difficult rock walls in Colorado, stated, "The highest individual achievements are never solo events...you only reach your best with the help of other people..."[5] Even some animals practice the power of teamwork. For example, though male lions do not usually participate in the hunt for food, the lionesses still get the job done by a system of cooperation. They hunt in groups or prides. The majority of the hunting group will chase their prey toward another group lying in wait. This group then engages in a short chase, leaps on the target, and makes the kill. Mission accomplished.

The Power of Cooperation

Deuteronomy 32:30 speaks of one chasing a thousand and two putting 10,000 to flight. The lesson to be learned is that two

> *There is not a single bodily activity or function that does not require the cooperation of another part of the body.*

working together as a team will be ten times more effective than one going solo. Teams create synergy. The best explanation of synergy is that a hand is more effective than five fingers working independent of each other. One day, while working out in my home gym, I decided to put this theory to the test. Using various free weights, I determined that two pounds was the most I could lift with a single finger. Once I established that fact, I then wanted to see how much weight I could lift with all of the fingers cooperating with each other. I rationalized that if I could lift two pounds per finger, then the obvious result using all five should be ten pounds. Not so. I was able to lift 35 pounds with a single hand. The teamwork created synergy.

The human body in general is by far the best example of true cooperation. There is not a single bodily activity or function that does not require the cooperation of another part of the body. I thought long and hard about this fact one day and decided to find one activity to refute this theory. I said to myself, "I'll just think, without moving a muscle." Within seconds I realized that I was breathing—a very necessary function to getting oxygen to the brain.

Now, in spite of the fact that David killed Goliath, he would have lost his life to another giant had it not been for the cooperation and intervention of another soldier.

> Once again there was a battle between the Philistines and Israel. David went down with his men to fight against the Philistines, and he became exhausted. And Ishbi-Benob, one of the descendants of Rapha, whose bronze spearhead weighed three hundred shekels and who was armed with a new sword, said he would kill

David. But Abishai son of Zeruiah came to David's rescue; he struck the Philistine down and killed him. Then David's men swore to him, saying, "Never again will you go out with us to battle, so that the lamp of Israel will not be extinguished" (2 Samuel 21:15-17).

No matter what kind of a reputation you may have earned, you will need the help of others to succeed. As actor Clint Eastwood in the movie *Dirty Harry* cautioned, "A man's got to know his limitations."

When the press interviewed Edmund Hillary regarding the key to his success in being the first to reach the top of Mount Everest, his response was inspiring:

> Without a doubt our greatest strength on Everest in 1953 was our very strong team spirit. Individually, as mountaineers, we were not particularly expert people. We were competent climbers, but we worked together, and we were determined that someone should get to the top. All of us, of course, wanted to be that one, but it was even more important that someone in the group reach the summit. In modern-day climbing, this team spirit is not quite so common. There are many more prima donnas in the modern climbing fraternity, people who have great skills and a great individualism but who may not work together as enthusiastically as we did.[6]

Harmoniously Different

Functioning effectively in a team does not mean that one has to sacrifice his individuality. There is a difference between cooperating and consolidating.

I get great delight from observing how well the musicians at my church perform as a team. When I have peeked in on their rehearsals, I often notice that the conductor does not hesitate to stop everything when a particular instrument is not in tune. The off-key musician takes no offense, for he knows he must

> *To be an effective team member, you must respect and value what others bring to the table.*

play in harmony with the others in order to achieve an excellent end product. And boy, excellence is what they produce! They are the best.

As a member of a team, you must place a high premium on the skills, talents, or other benefits *you* bring to the group. Your failure to perceive that your merchandise is good will rob you of your enthusiasm, your commitment, and your effectiveness. Further, to be an effective team member, you must respect and value what others bring to the table.

I once worked on a special management committee in a medium-sized corporation. Each person on the committee had emotional issues that caused him or her to be ineffective team members. The fact that I had more training, education, and exposure than they—coupled with the fact that I did not want to participate—really affected my attitude toward them. One team member was a yes-man who agreed with whatever the last person said; he never seemed to have an original thought. Another member of the team had been with the organization forever, had no exposure beyond its walls, and was thus inflexible and out of touch with the real world. The remaining three members were simply unqualified for their positions—which kept them in a defensive, never-accept-the-blame mode of operating. In retrospect, I realized I had developed a prima donna attitude of impatience and lack of respect for whatever input they timidly put forth. I simply nodded at their suggestions, knowing that if I did not follow through, the plans would never come to fruition.

One night when I submitted my frustrations with the group to the Lord, I realized that the key cause of my unhappiness was that I placed little or no value on their input. I decided then and there to began to look for the good in each person. I made note of the fact that Mr. Yes was indeed quite a pleasant individual and got along with everyone. He could be counted on for support even if he did not understand the issues. Mrs. Unexposed was too old and insecure to change and would continue to be a problem, but she was the sandpaper I needed to smooth the rough edges of my underdeveloped patience. She definitely contributed to my spiritual growth. The other team members really had a desire to learn but were very insecure because of their limited knowledge and unmarketable skills. Notwithstanding, they were good listeners. Occasionally, because of their longevity with the company, they provided good insight into the origin of certain operating problems.

It finally dawned on me that God had placed me in the company because of my experience in order to bring change. Being pompous and impatient would surely sabotage my divine assignment. With a new understanding of my purpose, I framed and posted in clear view in my office the passage found in 1 Corinthians 4:7: "For who makes you different from anyone else? What do you have that you did not receive? And if you did receive it, why do you boast as though you did not?"

I humbled myself and repented for my haughty attitude. I am convinced more and more each day that humility is the quickest path to the high places in God and to achieving our goals.

Humble Cooperation

I heard a story about two mountain goats who were coming from opposite sides of the mountain and met each other on a narrow ledge. The ledge was just wide enough for one of them to pass. On one side was the steep wall of the mountain and on the other side was a cliff. The two were facing each other, and there was no room to turn around and impossible for either to back up. How do you think they solved their dilemma?

If they had been certain people that I know, they would have started butting each other, insisting on their right to pass until they both fell off the cliff. But, as the story goes, these goats exercised more wisdom than that. Goat A decided to lie down and let Goat B literally walk over him. Consequently, they each resumed their trek and reached their destination. Sometimes we have to exercise a little humility to reach our goals. I know this concept flies in the face of our modern-day mind-set of looking out for number one, but I have learned the difference between letting someone walk *over* you versus walking *on* you. You can never be harmed or disadvantaged by someone stepping *over* you. No one can block your destiny. Now, only people with low self-evaluation will allow people to step *on* them. Walking over me will not diminish or disadvantage me. Goat A's decision to humble himself assured that he would reach *his* goal.

At a team-building seminar I attended some time ago, the leader kept admonishing us to remember that "none of us is as smart as all of us." I'm not sure if he authored the phrase, but I will never forget the reality of it. I repeat it often.

The Curse of Competition

Competition in personal relationships is futile and counterproductive; everybody loses. A defeat can reinforce the loser's existing insecurities while victory can cause the winner to base his security on the weak foundation of outdoing others. Many competitive people are insecure. They are obsessed with proving they are better than someone else in one endeavor or another. Merely *knowing* that they are better is not good enough. They must constantly prove it—primarily to themselves. Winning gives them worth.

Many people have a "scarcity" mind-set and believe there is only one pie out there in God's big world and that a slice for someone else means less for them. Such limited thinking is an insult to our Father, who has infinite resources. Some time ago, my friend Bunny Wilson took a sabbatical from her busy speaking and writing schedule. I was really impressed when, without hesitation, she recommended me and her other friends in the public speaking ministry to take her place at some of her recurring conferences. There are people who would compare such an act to giving your competitors a listing of your customers' names and addresses. But not Bunny. She walks in a high level of faith and emotional security. She steadfastly believes and often asserts that "whatever God has for you, you'll get it." The prophet Isaiah agreed. "For the LORD Almighty has purposed, and who can thwart him? His hand is stretched out, and who can turn it back?" (Isaiah 14:27).

A cooperative spirit will become the norm once we embrace the fact that we plant seeds for our own success when we support others. Take the case of Paul and Apollos. They could have been chief competitors in ministry. They were both educated and anointed men of God. In fact, some of the Christians at Corinth felt they had to choose sides as to which one to follow—despite the fact that they preached the same gospel. Paul took them to task for their carnal attitudes.

> When one of you says, "I am a follower of Paul," and another says, "I prefer Apollos," aren't you acting like those who are not Christians? Who is Apollos, and who is Paul, that we should be the cause of such quarrels? Why, we're only servants. Through us God caused you to believe. Each of us did the work the Lord gave us. My job was to plant the seed in your hearts, and Apollos watered it, but it was God, not we, who made it grow. The ones who do the planting or watering aren't important, but God is important because he is the one who makes the seed grow. The one who plants and the one who waters work as a team with the same purpose. Yet they will be rewarded individually, according to their own hard work. We work together as partners who belong to God. You are God's field, God's building—not ours (1 Corinthians 3:4-9 NLT).

Paul refused to get caught up in a popularity contest. His response was the complete opposite of what we witness today.

Many ministers make disparaging remarks about other ministries on radio and national television. It is such a turnoff to believers and nonbelievers. Unlike Diotrephes, the insecure, unsupportive leader whom we met in a previous chapter, Paul had no vain ambitions. His primary objective was to spread the gospel, and he wanted to make sure that no minister was hindered from doing so. In his letter to Titus, Paul encouraged believers to give Apollos their full support. "Do everything you can to help Zenas the lawyer and Apollos with their trip. See that they are given everything they need" (Titus 3:13 NLT). Such a request could only emanate from a secure heart.

For the child of God, an employer is merely a chosen channel for a chosen season.

One of the core values of my professional life has been that I will leave my promotion and "exaltation" to God. The apostle Peter admonished, "Therefore humble yourselves under the mighty hand of God, that He may exalt you in due time" (1 Peter 5:6 NKJV). This Scripture does not mean that we should not ask for what we want nor ardently pursue our goals. What it does mean is that we must refuse to engage in backstabbing, vying for favor, or any other worldly methods in order to get a promotion or advantage to ensure our success. God orchestrates the careers of His children. When He has ordained a promotion, nothing and no one can stop it—not even being thrown into a lion's den. Ask Daniel (see Daniel 6:1-28).

For those of you who work outside the home, know that it is an insult to your heavenly Father to think that a particular employer is your only source of provision. For the child of God, an employer is merely a chosen channel for a chosen season. When you get this truth ingrained in your heart, you will walk in total security in the workplace and become a real team player.

Team Building

If you are trying to build a team, you must be careful that as a leader you do not sabotage the group's effectiveness by catering to or rewarding prima donnas. Whether something good or bad happens, the entire team should share the glory or the pain. In the heartwarming movie *Coach Carter*, the no-nonsense high school basketball coach imposed an impossible physical training penalty on one of the talented but rebellious players who had quit the team because he did not want to submit to the coach's strict disciplines. After a time, the player missed the interaction of the group and the opportunity to be a part of a now-winning team. He wanted in again. The coach agreed to allow him to rejoin the team on one condition: He had to complete an extraordinary number of push-ups and "suicide runs" by a certain date. All of the exercises had to be done during regular team practice under the watchful eye of the coach's assistant. On the final day, the penitent student was not able to reach his goal. The wise coach told him to hit the road. At that moment, a funny thing happened. One by one, each member of the team, now understanding what it meant to work together, slowly volunteered to complete his requirement. The coach, heartened by their show of unity, allowed it and the player rejoined the team. The group went on to achieve unprecedented success.

> *Everybody on a championship team doesn't get publicity, but everyone can say he's a champion.*

For any team to maximize its potential, each member must be willing to subordinate his personal agenda to the team's agenda. In the end, everybody wins. Basketball great Earvin "Magic" Johnson once said, "Everybody on a championship team doesn't get publicity, but everyone can say he's a champion."

Of course, not every leader is like Coach Carter. I have seen insecure bosses deliberately create dissension among members of their staff. Obviously, they feared that if the employees worked in harmony, they would unite against them. Management is certainly not for cowards or insecure people.

CONFIDENCE CHALLENGE

⊘· On a scale of one to ten, ten being highest, how effective a team player are you?

⊘· Explain your score.

Engaging
Constructive Feedback

Whoever loves discipline loves knowledge,
but he who hates correction is stupid.

PROVERBS 12:1

O ONE HAS 20-20 VISION on himself, and no one exercises total objectivity in evaluating his own behavior. It is not the way of human nature. We all need feedback for personal growth and development. Because we all require it, we will often find ourselves challenged with being either the recipient or the giver of such helpful communication. Unfortunately, insecure people do not *seek* nor readily *give* constructive feedback. They are afraid of negative responses.

I had an interesting experience in the workplace once when I headed an editing committee whose responsibility was to make sure that the company's annual report of operations was a quality production. The report was a compilation of narratives written by various department managers. Being a team player and having been indoctrinated in the great benefits of feedback, my first action after writing my department's segment of the report was to have a certain group of my peers review it. No one made any suggestions for correction. Assuming that all those who had contributed to the report were working toward the same goal, the committee freely edited out bad grammar, misspellings, long complicated sentences, extraneous information, and all other violations of the rules of effective writing. Big mistake. Many of the contributors were offended by the modifications. Tempers flared. I was flabbergasted to see people who viewed corrections as personal attacks. I felt my career plane had just experienced a crash landing in "Insecurityville." Fortunately, God has so fortified my emotions through the various unpopular management positions I have held over the past 33 years that I jokingly refer to myself as the "Teflon Queen"—nothing sticks to me. God sustained me through that experience, and I thanked Him many times that I had been drilled during my career to always solicit a second pair of eyes on any worthwhile project. In a phrase made popular in the movie *The Godfather,* "It wasn't personal, just business."

We must have the confidence and the courage to provide meaningful input without fearing that someone will become upset and never speak to us again.

I watched a recent documentary on the career of U.S. Secretary of Defense Donald Rumsfeld. The commentator described him as a "lighting rod for criticism." He further noted that Rumsfeld had always had to make unpopular decisions during his political and professional career. The goal-oriented Rumsfeld stated, "If you are not criticized, you may not be doing much." He further declared, "It isn't making mistakes that's critical; it's correcting them and getting on with the principal task." Whether you agree with his politics or not, you must admit that these are clearly the words of a very secure man.

Giving Constructive Feedback

Giving constructive feedback can be perceived as either a negative or a positive undertaking. I believe that even if the feedback is negative in the sense of pointing out a shortcoming or needed area of improvement, the objective should always be to enhance or develop some aspect of a person's life or performance. Unfortunately, if the receiver has low self-worth, any pointing out of a weakness may be met with defensiveness, resentment, or even hostility. Consequently, most people are loath to saying anything at all. We have to remember that people are not like mushrooms; they cannot grow in the dark. They must be informed on how they are performing. We must have the confidence and the courage to provide meaningful input without fearing that someone will become upset and never speak to us again. If we really care about somebody, we must take the chance, for their sake, on helping them develop.

The story of Apollos provides a perfect example of how to give *and* receive constructive feedback. Apollos was an educated Jew who had a thorough knowledge of the Scriptures and the Jewish religion. He came to the city of Ephesus more than 50 years after the death of Christ. "He had been instructed in the way of the Lord, and he spoke with great fervor and taught about Jesus accurately, though he knew only the baptism of John. He began to speak boldly in the synagogue. When Priscilla and Aquila heard him, they invited him to their home and explained to him the way of God more adequately" (Acts 18:25-26).

Aquila and Priscilla were a husband-and-wife team who were fellow tentmakers and partners in ministry with the apostle Paul. Having listened to Apollos preach, it was apparent to them that despite his education, his eloquence, and his enthusiasm, there was one thing missing in his experience—an encounter with the Holy Spirit. They knew this component would make all the difference in the world in his ministry.

We have to applaud the spiritual maturity of this godly couple, who decided to help this young man be all that he could be for God. Rather than disparaging him to others, criticizing his deficiency, or envying his great oratory skills, they chose to invite him to their home and explain to him the full gospel of Christ. Had Apollos been a proud, conceited know-it-all, he would have rejected their counsel. Rather, he demonstrated humility and teachableness by submitting to their guidance. Fully equipped with the anointing—coupled with his adeptness in the Scriptures—Apollos became an even more valuable asset to the work of Lord. He "was a great help to those who by grace had believed. For he vigorously refuted the Jews in public debate, proving from the Scriptures that Jesus was the Christ" (Acts 18:27-28).

Practicing the Principles

The ability to provide constructive feedback is learned behavior. The more we practice it, the better we become at it. Let's look at four practical, God-honoring ways to provide helpful input.

Prayerfully. Pray before you decide to approach someone with constructive feedback. Ask God to reveal your true motive. Are you angry with the person and want to get something off your chest? Are you just being critical in order to make yourself feel better about your own shortcomings and insecurities? Once you are clear as to your motives, you must pray that the person will be receptive to your input. Think about what you will say. Get God's guidance. Believe that the words He will give you will have the right impact. "So is my word that goes out from my mouth: It will not return to me empty, but will accomplish what I desire and achieve the purpose for which I sent it" (Isaiah 55:11). It is usually when we approach someone with our own logic, judgment, or opinion that we run into resistance.

Promptly. Don't delay to give needed feedback. The situation will only continue, and maybe even get worse, when the person is not aware of his shortcoming. Aquila and Priscilla could easily have said, "We'll just pray for Apollos, and maybe God will reveal to him what he needs to know." A prompt conversation will enable you to more accurately cite specific instances of the problematic behavior. Of course, it would be helpful to be prepared to offer specific suggestions for improvement.

Personally. Go directly to the person yourself—always face-to-face when possible. No one appreciates knowing you have shared his shortcomings with everybody else in his circle of interaction before you told him. Own the problem. Tell him what you have observed personally. Don't hide behind what "they" are saying. Ideally, you will have already demonstrated your support toward the person long before you decide you need to "fix" him. This will certainly help him to be more receptive to your input.

Privately. Be sure that no one else is around to hear the feedback. Aquila and Priscilla did not confront Apollos in the courtyard of the synagogue; they taught him in the privacy of their home. Giving constructive feedback in the presence of others will only cause the person to be concerned with saving face; there is a good chance he will not absorb a word you say. Find a quiet place where you can discuss the issues without interruption.

Don't be disappointed if the person doesn't immediately embrace your feedback. Sometimes the truth is too painful to be accepted quickly. Express your care and support and leave the rest to God. You've done your job.

Receiving Constructive Feedback

No one enjoys hearing about his weaknesses. It was Job who said, "How painful are honest words" (Job 6:25). Receiving feedback, no matter how much it is designed to help, can be especially painful for insecure people. They interpret any mention of a need to improve as a confirmation or proof of their worst fears—they are lacking something.

If you are ever going to walk in confidence, then you must learn how to benefit from such input. Allow me to give you

> *Know that your defensiveness is often the resistance of your flesh to the pain of the truth.*

four tips for responding to not-so-pleasant information.

Listen. Do not interrupt with an explanation or excuse for your behavior. Know that your defensiveness is often the resistance of your flesh to the pain of the truth. "If you listen to constructive criticism, you will be at home among the wise" (Proverbs 15:31 NLT). Let your body language indicate that you are intent on hearing all that the person is saying to you. Avoid smirking, rolling your eyes, or seeming incredulous. Instead, try nodding your head, looking the confronter in his eyes, and asking clarifying questions. This will encourage the person to relax and not to search so hard for the right words to keep from offending you. Most of all, don't plan on how you will respond; just keep listening. Also, silently pray to discern hidden motives. Some people simply enjoy being critical. They can only feel good about themselves when they diminish others.

Look. Check to see if there is a kernel of truth. "Valid criticism is as treasured by the one who heeds it as jewelry made from finest gold" (Proverbs 25:12 NLT). There is usually some modicum of truth to negative input—especially when you hear it from more than one person. Don't be afraid of the truth. Truth will set you free. It is not your enemy; it will always be your friend. Remember the Arabian proverb that says, "If one person calls you a donkey, pay no attention to him. But if five people call you one, go and buy yourself a saddle."

Learn. Be open to new ways to behave. Ask for suggestions. Teachableness is a godly trait. "Instruct a wise man and he will be wiser still; teach a righteous man and he will add to his learning" (Proverbs 9:9). Apollos' ministry took a whole new direction when he embraced the truth that Aquila and Priscilla taught him.

Leave. You don't have to entertain groundless criticism. Simply say, "Thank you for your input." You handle feedback much the way you eat bony fish; you eat the flesh and leave the bones. Don't spend time rehearsing the encounter. Even Jesus didn't please everybody. We must adopt the attitude of the apostle Paul, "No, dear brothers and sisters, I am still not all I should be, but I am focusing all my energies on this one thing: Forgetting the past and looking forward to what lies ahead, I strain to reach the end of the race and receive the prize for which God, through Christ Jesus, is calling us up to heaven" (Philippians 3:13-14 NLT).

Paul admonished us to get dressed for spiritual success by putting on the whole armor of God. One of the most critical aspects of the armor is the shield of faith, for it protects us from the fiery darts of the enemy. Let all of the "confidence zapping" comments and accusations hurled your way hit your shield of faith rather than absorbing them into your emotions. I'm often reminded of the fact that no matter how much water you pour on a duck's back, it simply rolls off. We must keep our armor intact and not let criticism penetrate our soul, mind, will, or emotions.

CONFIDENCE CHALLENGE

- Write a brief script of what you will say to someone whom you have been planning or desiring to give constructive feedback.

- How you would feel or respond if you were the recipient of this input?

Establishing Boundaries

"If you do not obey these commands,"
declares the LORD, "I swear by myself
that this palace will become a ruin."

JEREMIAH 22:5

OD HAS BOUNDARIES. The Bible is replete with His commands and the consequences of not adhering to them. Establishing boundaries remains a popular topic in Christian circles these days, as many believers are beginning to understand that being a doormat does not make them more godly. Some people are so eager to belong that they will abandon their ideas, opinions, tastes, and preferences just to be in relationship with a particular person or group. You can never become a secure person if you feel you cannot be your own person; the real you has left home.

Setting Boundaries

In the past when I taught conflict resolution, I often asserted that some people had no boundaries. What I have come to realize over the years, however, is that we all have limits beyond which we do not want others to go. Some people are very direct in expressing those limits, while others are too fearful of rejection and alienation to communicate them. Sometimes even little annoyances, such as someone constantly mispronouncing your name or innocently teasing you, can go on for years if you never express your objection to it. Consider the story related to me by Ann.

Ann is a beautiful, dark-skinned African American who loves chocolate. One day a gentlemen who is also African American came onto her floor at work carrying chocolates for the entire staff. Ann expressed her excitement and dove right in to the goodies. When he came in the office a few weeks later, he greeted Ann very cheerily by saying, "Hello, Chocolate." While Ann has no personal insecurities about her deeply pigmented skin, she knew he was making a subtle reference to her complexion. She decided that she'd better nip the problem in the bud then and there. She very evenly said, "Sam, I'd prefer that you just call me Ann." Unsurprisingly, when she saw Sam some time later, he seemed a little distant. She knew he had been offended by her mild rebuke. Notwithstanding, he never called her "Chocolate" again. Ann's only other option in dealing with this situation would have been to allow him to continue to annoy her, and in so doing, to cause her to build resentment toward him. Setting boundaries can be a risky undertaking, and sometimes it requires real emotional security to take the plunge.

> *No one should ever make it a habit to sacrifice for anyone to the point of resentment. Not even God.*

Many insecure people say yes when they want to say no. They often make sacrifices for others to the point of resentment. This is a horrible mistake. No one should ever make it a habit to sacrifice for anyone to the point of resentment. Not even God. That's right, the Lord does not want us to serve Him grudgingly. The psalmist admonishes us to "serve the LORD with gladness" (Psalm 100:2 KJV).

Closing the Door

If you want to accelerate your growth in the area of setting boundaries, you must immediately begin saying no to activities that bring you no enjoyment and that do not fit in to your divine purpose for your life. In an earlier chapter, we discussed the story of how Jesus refused to mediate a property dispute between two brothers. When one of them interrupted His teaching to ask Him to intervene regarding their inheritance, Jesus simply replied, "Man, who appointed me a judge or an arbiter between you?" (Luke 12:14). In other words, Jesus was saying, "I'm not going to allow you to distract Me from My purpose by getting involved in something I have not been called to do." The additional lesson to be learned from the incident is that Jesus didn't give a long explanation as to why He couldn't oblige them. Further, He did not say He wasn't available right now but would try to get back with them later. Such a response always leaves the door open for a subsequent request. He simply gave a firm and final no and closed the door permanently on the issue.

Has someone ever asked you to lend them some money and you responded, "I'm sorry that I don't have it this time"? What do you think would have happened if you had said, "Sally, I'm not going to lend you the money because I realize that I am enabling you to continue to spend irresponsibly, which is not helping you"?

To be quite honest, I'm still not totally comfortable saying no without an explanation. Many years ago I would volunteer from time to time to babysit some rather raucous kids from our church. My goal was to relieve a friend who had been manipulated into hosting them more frequently than she desired. I knew she really needed my support since she was much older than I and was also responsible for the care of her ailing husband. After a while, the parents of these children started to request my services directly—even during times I had set aside for my husband. I found myself searching for a legitimate excuse to give as to why I could not accommodate their request. On one occasion, my husband, overhearing me on the phone trying to wiggle out of the now-dreaded task, called from the background, "You don't need to explain. Just say that you don't want to babysit!" As I later reflected on my reluctance to be so straightforward, I realized I was afraid of falling out of favor with this couple. They held an influential position at church, and I felt privileged to be in relationship with them. Of course, this was many years ago. Today I would, without hesitation, quickly inform them of exactly when or if I would be available.

> *Boundaries without consequences are just wishes.*

If you are just starting to develop your sense of security, you may be more comfortable responding to an undesirable request by stating, "I'm sorry. I have a prior commitment." You may be asking, "Suppose I do not have a commitment?" Indeed you do. You have made a commitment to yourself to stop being manipulated into doing things you do not want to do.

Boundaries and Consequences

As we become secure enough to establish our personal boundaries, we must also go a step further and express the consequences we are willing to implement when someone violates them. Now, this may sound a little harsh but boundaries without consequences are just wishes. Wishes will not change anybody's behavior toward us. It is sad to watch parents who constantly threaten to punish their children for wayward behavior but never follow-through with it. My father never made empty promises about the consequences of our disobedience. In fact, his threats and follow through usually occurred simultaneously! Boy, did he put the fear of consequences in us.

Christians who believe that mercy should endure forever deem it ungodly to impose consequences. Perhaps we should

take a quick look at a few of God's boundaries and related consequences:

- Behold, all souls are Mine…the soul who sins shall
  die (Ezekiel 18:4 NKJV).

- "If you do not listen, and if you do not set your
  heart to honor my name," says the LORD Almighty,
  "I will send a curse upon you, and I will curse your
  blessings" (Malachi 2:2).

- For if you forgive men when they sin against you,
  your heavenly Father will also forgive you. But if
  you do not forgive men their sins, your Father will
  not forgive your sins (Matthew 6:14-15).

God makes it very clear that when we violate His boundaries, there will indeed be consequences. The choice is ours.

Just as God has established a boundary on the ocean waters
so that the tide only comes in so far (Job 38:8-11), so must we
set limits on how far we let people go in interacting with us.

I had a high school teacher who always said, "One man's
rights end where another's begin." Boundaries help us to define
the parameters of our lives. Setting them in our personal and
professional lives is a godly thing to do.

I once took a job at a company that had very loose time card
procedures. When I came on board as the controller, the har-
ried payroll clerk was on the verge of an emotional breakdown
trying to keep up with the variety of time reporting methods
which included memos, ineffectively designed time sheets, and
special work sheets. Why, some of the executives refused to
submit a time sheet at all. This made it impossible to track their
vacation and sick time balances. It was clear to me that the
place was in need of structure. I immediately developed a standard time sheet and announced that all employees who desired
a paycheck would be required to submit the proper time sheet
in a timely manner and accurately filled out. The announcement

went over like a skunk at a picnic. A few of the executives tested my boundaries and did not comply initially. I then informed everyone I would assume that those who failed to submit the new time sheet had elected to enroll in my "deferred compensation" plan; that is, their check would be deferred until we received the time sheet. This consequence yielded unanimous compliance. Of course, I didn't win many friends, but the chaos stopped and I achieved my goal of a payroll that was done in an orderly manner and in compliance with state labor laws.

When we fail to express our boundaries, people become unclear as to what behavior will be accepted or tolerated by us. They are left to decide for themselves based upon their own preferences, convenience, or whims.

Life's Stewardship Boundaries

God has made us stewards over three key areas of our lives where the lines of interaction can become fuzzy if we do not clearly define them. Let's look at them.

Our time. Time discriminates against no one. Whether rich or poor, thin or fat, educated or not, we all get 1440 minutes each day. If we do not structure our days according to our desired priorities, we will constantly find ourselves frustrated and wondering where our time went.

I recall a time when I had an open-door policy at my office. My goal was to offer good customer service to the department heads by being available to address their financial and other concerns within my realm of responsibility. This policy turned my office into a beehive of activity. There would be times where as many as three or four people would be literally standing in my office waiting their turn to see me. I felt like Moses in the wilderness trying to address the problems of each person in the multitude on a daily basis. The lines were frustrating them and me. I did not need a Jethro to tell me that the thing that I was doing was not good (see Exodus 18). It was obvious. I brought my policy to a screeching halt. I immediately required everyone to make an appointment before coming to my office. Some managers initially refused to honor my request, and would saunter in to discuss their issues anyway. Because I worked with my door open most of the time, they assumed I was available. They had no regard for the fact that I had to process my own endless to-do list. I finally had to start working with my door closed. I posted a sign requesting all visitors to make an appointment first. I insisted that my assistant enforce my boundary without respect of persons. I overheard one manager complain that I, as chief financial officer, was trying to be more important than the chief executive officer. Still, I stuck to my guns until I established order in my environment.

I find that people in general do not embrace new structure or change. Does this mean we should allow chaos or disorganization to continue so we can avoid being unpopular with others? God forbid! In my situation, I repeatedly explained that when they honored my time boundary, it allowed me to serve them more effectively by giving them my undivided attention.

On the home front, I waged another war with time boundaries. My husband is an early riser and asks that during the week, people refrain from calling our home after 10 P.M. Now, I have some single friends and forgetful family members who know that I am a night owl and can usually be found working at my computer quite late. When they ignored our boundary and called the house anyway, I immediately reminded them that they were calling past the phone curfew time. If they violated the boundary again, I did not answer the phone. I used the answering machine to screen out the call and later told them I did so because it was past the curfew. Of course, I could have chosen to say nothing and become resentful—but that would not be good for me or them since it would have eventually eroded our relationship.

Our talent. It is personally rewarding and esteem-boosting to know you have a skill or talent other people need and desire. However, it can also be a source of frustration when others conclude that they have a right to *freely* use your talent simply for the asking.

I have a friend whom we will call Joyce who is a very talented singer. She has done backup work for well-known entertainers but has never really broken into the big times. Notwithstanding, singing is one of her various sources of financial support. Retreat and event organizers have been known to call her and ask if she would sing without compensation. Some have informed her, "We pay the speakers but not the singers." Others have offered to pay for her lodging and travel expenses only. She is infuriated by their presumptuousness. When she relates the incidents to me, she says, "What makes them think I just want a vacation?" Or she will say, "I choose the charities I want to give my time to. No one else can decide that for me." It would do Joyce well to establish a fee schedule along with other engagement requirements. If she is uncomfortable discussing her fees, she could pay a friend or someone else a modest fee on a per-event basis to handle this aspect of the business for her. Establishing an official business name for her services would also imply that her services are for *hire*. Joyce should also remind her darling family members, who are proud of her talent, to refrain from sending her nonpaying referrals; this happens often.

As a CPA I receive numerous calls requesting financial services I could indeed render if I wanted to work 24 hours a day. Some are from old acquaintances or friends of friends who are hoping I will do the work pro bono. Occasionally, I will volunteer my lunchtime for one hour of brain-picking. However, I have found that people place little value on anything gotten too cheaply. Therefore, I have developed a list of professionals who can accommodate their needs.

Boundaries will keep us emotionally and physically healthy. We do not have to express them in a mean-spirited way. It is not an either-or proposition. Rather, it is a matter of deciding what you want or don't want for your life.

Our treasure. The financial arena is one of the most challenging areas of setting boundaries. It is no secret that the majority of marriages fail because of financial issues. Long-term relationships can be dissolved when someone fails to repay a personal loan. The following advice on setting financial boundaries is an excerpt from my book *Show Me the Money!*

- Discuss with your spouse the maximum dollar amount that each of you may spend without getting the other's permission. Any amount above this limit will be considered "major" and will require complete agreement. Every couple defines a "major purchase" differently depending on their household income. Stick to what has been agreed on. Trust me—this is important. If you do not get in agreement on a transaction, when the deal goes bad the tendency is to point fingers.

- Advise your family that personal loans are against your "house policy." Should you decide to make an exception to the policy, make sure your spouse is in complete agreement. Put terms and due dates in writing.

- Don't enable your child, spouse, or anyone else to remain irresponsible by bailing him out or always being his safety net. Just say no. By not saying no, you interrupt one of God's most effective principles—sowing and reaping the consequences of individual behavior. Real maturity occurs when this lesson is learned. Love must be tough! If you are an enabler, ask God right now to give you the strength to stop being so. Insist on that rent check for your still-at-home adult child. This is real love.[7]

Some individuals love the attention they receive from serving or giving to others with a martyr's attitude. I know people who let others violate their boundaries by borrowing money or manipulating them to perform other favors. When I hear some say something like, "I gave Mary my last dollar!" I have to resist the temptation to say, "Who forced you to do it? What's your payoff? Is the sympathy or attention you want of greater value to you than your cash? Stop the charade. God loves a cheerful giver. Whatever you give, you must give out of a pure heart or God has no further reward for you."

I have an over-50 relative whose sense of worth is inextricably tied to giving money to others. He often finds himself in dire financial straits, living from paycheck to paycheck even though he makes a handsome salary. When he was growing up, his father was quite frugal and did not choose to give an allowance to each of his seven kids. They settled for the nickel or dime he gave them from time to time whenever they mustered enough courage to ask for it. The man in this example related a story to me of how one day his uncle gave him an entire quarter. He had never felt so happy in his life; he felt deep love for his uncle because of his extreme generosity. He vowed that one day he was going to be able to evoke that same feeling in somebody's child. Today he freely—sometimes foolishly—gives his money, food, and other favors to the children in his neighborhood who crowd around his car. They love to see him coming. I know that many times he cannot afford it, but he cannot risk the loss of their "love" by saying no to their pleas for money. He feels he must fill every gap left by irresponsible or absentee parents. My heart's desire is that he will seek counseling to deal with his erroneous beliefs and his false sense of responsibility.

Yes, setting time, talent, or treasure boundaries is an extremely problematic task for those of you who are insecure. But it doesn't have to be. You can break the habit of doing more and more things you do not really want to do—and hating every moment of it. The key is to start small with an issue you perceive has very little risk of loss or impact on the respective relationship. It may be as simple as deciding to only pay your small share of a restaurant bill rather than splitting the entire thing with fellow friends or family who ordered as if there were no tomorrow.

CONFIDENCE CHALLENGE

- In what area of your life do you need to set a boundary?

- Why haven't you done so? What do you really fear?

HABIT 5

Empowering Others

When Jesus had called the Twelve together,
he gave them power and authority to drive out all demons
and to cure diseases, and he sent them out
to preach the kingdom of God and to heal the sick.

LUKE 9:1-2

MOTIONALLY SECURE PEOPLE seek to empower others. Jesus was a master at it. By empowering His disciples, He ensured that His mission on earth would continue to be accomplished long after He was gone. To empower means to fill with power. Power is energy. When we make it a habit of empowering others, we energize them to reach their goals and ours. Jesus practiced this principle. "Verily, verily, I say unto you, he that believeth on me, the works that I do shall he do also; and greater works than these shall he do; because I go unto my Father" (John 14:12 KJV).

Successful retailers know that when they empower front line clerks to resolve customers' needs, they have created a win-win situation. Therefore, they readily give autonomy and flexibility in decision making. The results are repeat customers who enjoy the no-hassle policy and clerks who feel more empowered in their jobs.

Some managers, on the other hand, use lack of empowerment as a means for controlling their employees. Unfortunately, these managers have not learned how to multiply their effectiveness by making others more powerful. The principles of empowerment work the same in our personal lives and our work world.

There are several strategies for empowering others. Let's look at a few.

Inform/Train

There is nothing more demoralizing, disempowering, and esteem robbing than being kept out of the loop on information that impacts you. As difficult as it must have been to get His disciples to understand, Jesus knew He had to inform them of events to come that would affect them.

> Leaving that region, they traveled through Galilee. Jesus tried to avoid all publicity in order to spend more time with his disciples and teach them. He said to them, "The Son of Man is going to be betrayed. He will be killed, but three days later he will rise from the dead" (Mark 9:30-32 NLT).

Later He told them, "In my Father's house are many rooms; if it were not so, I would have told you. I am going there to prepare a place for you. And if I go and prepare a place for you, I will come back and take you to be with me that you also may be where I am. You know the way to the place where I am going" (John 14:2-4).

Being kept in the dark on key issues sabotages productivity and creativity.

If we accept the truism "information is power," you would think that everybody would use this tool to empower others. Unfortunately, some people withhold information as a means of controlling others. They use uncertainty to keep the employee guessing about his plight. Being kept in the dark on key issues sabotages productivity and creativity.

In the workplace, employees who receive company-sponsored training tend to be more loyal and productive. Such an investment in them gives them a sense of being valued and thereby meets one of the basic human needs. When they feel good about themselves, they will feel good about the company and seek ways to return the favor.

Needing to be informed is not limited to the workplace. Many stay-at-home wives do not feel empowered, as some of them have no knowledge of and no say in the family finances. I have counseled couples where the husband keeps his spendthrift wife in the dark on the extent of the household income rather than dealing directly with the issue of her irresponsibility. Both spouses need to be involved with major financial decisions and have a general understanding of monthly income and expenditures. More than half of all divorces are attributable to financial issues because one or both spouses have no clue how a partnership is supposed to work. In a business partnership, there has to be full disclosure to all partners if the entity is to survive.

> *Empowerment is simply loosing the reins over how something is going to be done while retaining control over what should be done.*

Trust

Empowerment occurs when you trust people with a task without micromanaging them. Empowerment is simply loosing the reins over *how* something is going to be done while retaining control over *what* should be done. Corporate management gurus all agree that employees perform better when given freedom to perform their jobs with some level of independence. They will begin to feel ownership of the project, the job, or the function. I am always careful to listen for a "we" versus "they" attitude when employees refer to their company or group. Their words are a surefire indication of how much empowerment they feel. Have you ever requested an item at a retail clothing store only to be told by the clerk, "I'm sorry, *I'm* out of that item"? Her words indicated that she has embraced ownership. On the other hand, I have been to other establishments where the clerks will often say, "I don't know when *they* will have that product available." No ownership; just a hired hand.

I worked with a manager who was so insecure that she did not trust her employees to engage in a conversation with another manager without her approval. Not only was she afraid her employees might cast her or the department in a negative light, she also feared they might form an allegiance with another manager. And yet she would often call employees from other departments into her office without consulting their managers. It was no wonder that her employees did things by rote and were reluctant to suggest needed changes to their departmental operations. They did not even have enough autonomy to have a conversation at will.

In a marriage, a wise woman empowers her husband when she demonstrates that she trusts his decision making. One of my mentors, considering my strong personality, gave me some sage advice early in my marriage on how to empower my husband. She warned, "Whatever you do, he won't do." What she meant was that if you want a man to be strong in an area, you must resist the temptation to take it over and handle it for him. This was some of the best input I have ever received. As a certified public accountant, it seemed only logical that I would handle our household finances. However, I really wanted my husband to lead and to be strong in this area. I did as she instructed. I earnestly prayed that God would give him wisdom. My great fear was that, since he had a more balanced view of life and loved to enjoy it, he might put a higher priority on a "fun invest-ment" than on savings or investing in productive assets. By the grace of God, I never negated a single financial decision that he made. Today he handles our finances with such proficiency that I find myself perplexed by some of the technicalities of online banking, computer-generated checks, and personal finance soft-ware programs. Had I chosen not to relinquish control, this complicated task would still be my responsibility.

Care

Showing that you care about people beyond what they can do for you is an act of empowerment. In these modern times of downsizing, rightsizing, and precipitous cutbacks to achieve bottom-line results, employee loyalty is at an all-time low. While you may have no direct control over certain company decisions, if you are a manager or supervisor, the least you can do is to show your staff that you care.

I conduct a weekly prayer meeting with my staff. We pray about their personal concerns, such as housing needs, car pur-chases, and so forth. I give them short presentations on negoti-ating mortgages, managing personal finances, and other areas unrelated to the job. When I come across information that is rel-evant to issues an employee may be facing, I bring it to him. The 20 minutes that I invest in this process are the most productive use of time I could make. It has brought cohesiveness to a team that was once unstable and contentious. Employees who have been quiet and withdrawn are now asking for help and expressing their personal needs.

Appreciate

I often muse over the fact God made us in His image. There-fore, I believe we share many of His desires. For instance, He wants us to praise, thank, and appreciate Him for His goodness. One of the frequently cited admonitions for us to do so is found in Psalm 100:4-5: "Enter his gates with thanksgiving and his courts with praise; give thanks to him and praise his name. For the LORD is good and his love endures forever; his faithfulness continues through all generations."

Now, how many of us want to be praised, thanked, and appreciated for the good we have done? It is a God-given desire. Hardly anything is more demoralizing than feeling unappreciated. I have watched sincere praise energize a person and cause him to spring up like a wilted flower that's just been watered. Since I have been on a campaign to appreciate good workers and to express my belief in their skills and abilities, I have received cards, gifts, and favors in return. I wish I had employed this strategy years ago rather than thinking that a paycheck should have been a good enough motivator.

I have also begun the habit of leaving friends and family members voice mails just expressing how grateful I am to have them in my life and giving specific praise for things they have done or for things I admire about them. One friend told me she kept the message on her answering machine so that she could replay it for occasional encouragement.

Oh, the dividends that a husband or wife or anyone else would reap from expressing appreciation for the little things. Just in case your gratitude muscle has grown weak and you take most kindnesses and efforts for granted, consider the list below as a starter for some possible tasks or responsibilities to appreciate your spouse for performing:

> Taking out the trash
> Filling the car with gasoline
> Buying the groceries
> Washing/folding the clothes
> Bathing the kids
> Being on time
> Watering the grass or plants

Sending out the Christmas cards
Preparing meals
Getting the car washed
Paying the bills
Going to work
Spending wisely
Selecting family birthday presents
Cleaning the house or room
Supporting your career
Being accountable
Listening

This list could go on and on. Why not set a goal of appreciating at least one thing per day for a particular person in your life? If you are a man, don't be so insecure that you fear you will appear weak if you start to notice the little things. It takes a real man to look beyond his needs and recognize the efforts of another.

When you walk in emotional security, you look for ways to give people more power by keeping them informed, trusting them, caring about them, or appreciating them. It will bring greater balance to your life as well as raise the esteem and productivity of the empowered one.

CONFIDENCE CHALLENGE

⊝· What fear has kept you from empowering someone in your circle of interaction?

⊝· What will you do today to start the process?

Enjoying Success

*It is not that we think we can do
anything of lasting value by ourselves.
Our only power and success come from God.*

2 CORINTHIANS 3:5 NLT

ID YOU KNOW you do not have to be emotionally secure to become successful? In fact, insecurity is often the catalyst that drives many to achieve. Their success becomes the antidote that diverts attention away from whatever it is that causes them to feel inadequate. Such high achievers have often succeeded out of fear of poverty, fear of repeating a parent's fate, fear of disappointing the expectations of family or friends, or fear of an endless list of other things. What I have learned, however, is that emotional security is essential if one is to maintain the freedom required to enjoy his success.

Fear of Success

Fear of success probably derails as many dreams as the fear of failure. I have talented, creative friends who could be making significant sums of money each year, but instead they find themselves living beneath their privileges, constantly battling the Internal Revenue Service or forever ending up on the wrong end of a deal. I cannot help but marvel at their ability to sabotage the success that should be theirs. They don't seem to be satisfied unless they are strapped financially. While I do not believe that success and wealth are inextricably linked, in this chapter we will assume that prosperity is one of the key by-products of accomplishing one's goals. Because I cannot be certain of the exact nature of my friends' particular fears, I can only surmise that they fall into one or more of the categories we will discuss below.

Fear of alienation by peers. From first grade to high school, I was blessed to make excellent grades. While I enjoyed the praises of my teachers, the fear of being isolated by my peers always cast a shadow on my achievements. I knew that most people assumed that if you excelled you would soon become "stuck up" and think that you were "all that." I had heard students whisper that other achievers thought they were "something." The price one paid for excelling was often alienation and rejection. For me, being an extremely sociable person, this was the ultimate punishment. I made sure I always downplayed my achievements and maintained relationships with a significant number of nonachievers. The same fear always lurked in my mind when I accomplished anything as an adult. I knew success could be alienating, so I tried to act as if I was never really that excited about anything I had done.

Peers will often raise their financial expectations of you once they know that your income has significantly increased. They may assume that you will pick up the tab when you dine with them—after all, you can afford it. It takes a secure person not to cave in to such pressure. It is best not to set a precedent by doing so. Do you have the courage to plop down only your portion of the bill and keep talking as if it is the most natural thing in the world? Or do you later agonize over what your friends thought about your action? Succeeding is not for the insecure.

Fear of isolation by family members. I am fortunate to belong to a very large and supportive family. I can readily share any achievement with them, and they love to brag about me to anybody who will listen. On the other hand, if someone grew up in a family where he was always the low man on the totem pole or the least likely to achieve, some family members might resent his rise to the top or even make assumptions about how he should interact with the family (especially financially) in light of his success. The thought of being held hostage to their expectations can be quite scary. Some people's insecurity will cause them to doubt if it is even worth pursuing their goals.

Fear of inability to maintain success. Being successful can create its own anxiety. I have a friend who wrote several chart-topping songs early in her career. She tells the story of the terrible anxiety she experienced when she was bombarded with thoughts that she might not be able to maintain her success. In fact, her anxiety became so severe that she was forced to seek professional help. Oh, that we could discipline ourselves to live in the now and to enjoy today. Winston Churchill said, "Success is never final, failure is never fatal."

Fear of attracting insincere people. Your success will draw many people who will get their self-worth from saying that they have a relationship with you. Solomon warned, "Wealth brings many friends, but a poor man's friend deserts him" (Proverbs 19:4).

It is important with each level of success to make every effort to continue to embrace your *real* friends, even though you may have outpaced them socially and financially. Be sensitive when discussing where you have traveled or the latest designer item that you purchased. Pray they will not become envious and resentful of your success. Share with them your sincere desire to stay connected. Prove it by including them where possible in some of your upscale activities and, most of all, in making time to do some of the things you used to do. Avoid being a show-off when you invite your old friends to your home. Why insist upon them developing a taste for caviar when you know you have always enjoyed fried chicken together?

Fear of being bombarded with financial requests. This fear is probably one of the most likely to come to fruition. My heart goes out to those celebrities who cannot enjoy an outing, even at church, without someone handing them a proposal or asking for a financial favor. Sure, we all know that to whom much is given, much will be required. And yes, success and wealth do indeed carry a heavy responsibility—but not to every Tom, Dick, and Harry who has "the idea of the century." No one should have to live like a hermit to have a peaceful existence. It takes real emotional security to say no and not worry about the bad publicity or unpopular image you may develop as a result. That's where trust in God must take center stage in your life. You must follow your heart, give as He directs, and leave your image up to Him. Of course, it is a good idea to establish a policy and boundaries on how you will deal with family and finances. If you are constantly inundated with requests from outsiders, you might consider getting a post office box strictly for such requests. Have business cards printed, and when approached, ask the person to mail the proposal to the address on the card and to expect a response from your representative within the next 90 days. Who knows, one proposal may be a real winner. Just keep in mind that you own nothing anyway. God entrusts you with money to manage for His glory.

Consider the story of John D. Rockefeller. His wealth almost proved to be his physical undoing. At 53 years old, Rockefeller earned around a million dollars a week, making him the only billionaire in the world. Unfortunately, his wealth could not cure his poor health. He was a very sick man who had to live on a very boring diet of milk and crackers. Sleep eluded him as he constantly worried about his money. Solomon said that there would be days like this for the rich. "The sleep of a laborer is sweet, whether he eats little or much, but the abundance of a rich man permits him no sleep" (Ecclesiastes 5:12). It seemed that Rockefeller's days were numbered. Then he discovered the secret to real success. He started pouring his money out to the needy. In turn, God poured health back into his body. He improved dramatically and lived to the ripe old age of 98. God wants us to enjoy His wealth His way.

The Relativity of Wealth

Wealth is relative. Someone will always have more and someone will always have less than you. It takes a daily, conscientious effort to fight discontentment and to enjoy whatever level of success you have already achieved. Everything around you from commercials, infomercials, and freeway billboards to well-meaning family and friends will scream, "You're lacking something. Buy this, buy that!"

As a pastime, my husband and I used to drive through Beverly Hills to look at the awesome houses there. Though God has blessed us and we live quite comfortably, we would often return home frustrated by the extreme wealth of those whose resources far exceeded our own. We would lament over the success of the "wicked" and encourage ourselves with the self-righteous conclusion that, in the final analysis, we were much better off than they, for we were faithful tithers and honored God with our money—as if none of them did! (There are many who do.) Ironically, we would often hear that someone had come to our home and experienced similar frustration with their plight when they saw us enjoying God's abundance. Oh, for the spirit of contentment to flood our hearts. Life would be such a joy.

Embracing the Success of Others

Some folks are too insecure to applaud the success or achievements of another, be it a coworker, distant relative, sibling, spouse, or even son or daughter. Their scarcity mentality causes them to feel they must have comparable success in order not to feel inferior. If they can indeed claim a similar personal achievement, then they are quick to mention it. For example,

Sue may tell her friend, "I'm glad you enjoyed your trip to Europe. Now, South Africa is the ultimate place to go. We had a ball there!" When they cannot point to a similar personal achievement, they often compete vicariously by mentioning another person's experience or achievement. The substituted person may be their child, friend, or any other acquaintance. For example, take the case of Lucy, who invited Janet to come over and see her newly remodeled kitchen. Upon seeing it, Janet exclaims, "Oh, you should see my friend Betty's new home. Her kitchen is awesome!" What Janet is really saying is, "My house does not compare to yours, but someone I'm associated with has a house that can compete with yours."

Catch yourself in action and resist the temptation to compete vicariously.

If you find yourself feeling the need to compete when a compliment is given to another, immediately recognize and renounce the spirit of insecurity that is trying to ensnare you. Catch yourself in action and resist the temptation to compete vicariously. Begin to reject this kind of behavior by responding in the opposite manner.

Practice being secure enough to enjoy someone else's achievements. I say "practice" because there is a good chance you will not "feel" secure initially. Just do it. Allow your faith to dictate your behavior. Faith without action or works is dead. I'm totally convinced that when you obey the Spirit and allow Him to determine your actions, the flesh grows weaker and weaker and must ultimately succumb to the control of the Spirit.

The Cloud of Envy

One of the unfortunate pitfalls of success is that many people are so filled with envy at your good fortune that they do not want you to enjoy it. Someone once said, "Few men have the strength to honor a friend's success without envy." It is understandable that many successful people choose to find new friends who do not make them feel guilty for having worked hard, paid their dues, and reaped the benefits—all by the grace of God.

If you do not develop your own sense of entitlement to what God has blessed you with, no one else will. I struggled with the concept of entitlement when I worked for a Fortune 500 company. I was part of a select group chosen to meet regularly with a popular psychiatrist whose assignment it was to make sure that we developed and maintained the right attitudes about success. We were periodically excused from our normal workday to attend the special training. The psychiatrist explained that upper management had targeted the individuals in our group for special treatment as part of corporate succession planning. I was not comfortable with the fact that others had to work while I sat there being enlightened on how to get ahead in corporate America. I had the naive mind-set that everything should be fair and that the favor we were receiving was somehow ungodly. It was not until years later that I realized that favor is not necessarily fair. In fact, the essence of the word "favor" implies that one is to be preferred over another. God promised to surround His children with favor. "For surely, O LORD, you bless the righteous; you surround them with your favor as with a shield" (Psalm 5:12). While I am to always be fair in my behavior towards others, I cannot reject the favor God sends my way just to keep others from becoming envious. We must began to embrace the success God has given to us as part of our destiny.

Success Anxiety

It is a tragedy to overcome all of the fears and obstacles to success only to have your accomplishments become a source of frustration and unhappiness.

Success anxiety and happiness anxiety are closely related. I remember after our first year of marriage how I grew anxious that Darnell and I had not had a big blowout argument so typical of young couples trying to merge their preferences, beliefs, finances, and other aspects of their lives. I was particularly bothered by our harmony since I grew up in a tumultuous household where peace and effective communication only existed in my fantasies. Our transition from singleness to oneness defied the marriage odds and divorce statistics I often read about with great interest and foreboding. I knew that my upbringing put me in the category of one unlikely to have a long-term marriage. I found it really scary that my husband and I actually flowed like best friends. I kept waiting for the *other* shoe to drop, after all, the first one had dropped while I lived at home.

Finally, no longer being able to stand the tranquility, I asked Darnell, "When are we going to have the Big One?" Perplexed, he asked, "The big what?" "You know, the big blowout argument." He looked me squarely in the eyes and very tenderly assured me that he was not, nor ever would be, the person that I feared he would become. I decided to give myself permission to be happy without feeling that it was a betrayal to my mother if my experience did not parallel hers. Somehow, I had internalized her subtle message that no one could be happily married. I felt she wanted us to have that in common. That was almost 26 years ago, and I am still happily married to my best friend.

It seems hard to imagine, but I know my story is not unique. I have had friends confide that they have to downplay their happiness to avoid disappointing a parent or other close relative bent on having marital misery in common with them.

Success anxiety happens pretty much the same way. Perhaps there was a parent or person who had significant influence in your life who was not able to overcome the obstacles to his or her success. They told you that you should never expect to be successful because of some legitimate-sounding reason they gave you at the time. However, you ignored their caution, worked hard, and achieved your goals. Unfortunately, you forgot to turn off the tape recorder in your mind that told you not to violate their expectation. Even though you may now be successful, you may feel that you do not deserve your good fortune and that it won't last. You may find yourself engaging in self-sabotaging behavior that will confirm your own fears and bring them to fruition.

What should you do? First, thank God that you understand the root of the problem. Second, talk it out with a good listener. Talking is therapy, and it often helps to release the problem of some of its potency. You already know that your thinking is flawed. Sometimes you just need someone, not always a professional therapist, to tell you so. Happiness is a choice. You are an independent, thinking adult now with a personal destiny that is not dependent on anyone else's experience. As you hear yourself put the problem in perspective, you may find yourself regularly declaring the words of Solomon, "Good advice and success belong to me. Insight and strength are mine" (Proverbs 8:14 NLT).

CONFIDENCE CHALLENGE

⌐· Have you ever found yourself minimizing your accomplishments or blessings in order to avoid creating envy or disappointing someone?

⌐· Are you now willing to embrace and enjoy your success?

Experiencing Peace

Peace I leave with you; my peace I give you.
I do not give to you as the world gives.
Do not let your hearts be troubled and do not be afraid.

JOHN 14:27

PEACE OF MIND IS the most valuable commodity in the world. Nothing can compare to it. Everyone desires inner peace but many fail to find it, for they seek for it in the wrong places. Jesus said that the peace He gives would not come in the same form as that of the world...fame, success, friends, promotion, power, attention, money, and bigger or more possessions. Nothing external will ever produce peace of mind. The uncertainties of modern living can keep us in a state of anxiety about real and imagined fears.

Emotional security and peace are inextricably linked. Peace is the absence of anxiety; insecure people are plagued with anxiety and a myriad of fears. When you interact with them, their self-consciousness, competitiveness, or self-promotion all reveal their inner fears. Even though they may don a facade of confidence, the person who is spiritually discerning can see right through their mask.

When we remember that the root meaning of "confidence" is "with faith," we realize there can be no confidence or peace without faith in an unfailing and loving Father.

Using the word "PEACE" as an acronym, let's take a brief look at some of the basic requirements for inner tranquility.

P—Prioritize Every Aspect of Your Life According to God's Word

When the Pharisees asked Jesus what the most important commandment of the law was, He replied, "Love the Lord your God with all your heart and with all your soul and with all your mind. This is the *first* and greatest commandment" (Matthew 22:37-38, emphasis added). The soul is comprised of the mind, the will, and the emotions; that's where peace abides.

There are two aspects of our lives where we must put first things first if we are to experience peace: finances and relationships. Peace comes from knowing we have done that.

Finances. Obeying God's financial priorities will eliminate anxiety and insecurity about your future ability to maintain the wealth you have gained as a result of your success. When you disobey, it weakens your faith muscle. "Blessed are those who trust in the LORD and have made the LORD their hope and confidence. They are like trees planted along a riverbank, with roots that reach deep into the water. Such trees are not bothered by the heat or worried by long months of drought. Their leaves stay green, and they go right on producing delicious fruit" (Jeremiah 17:7-8 NLT). It is when you have heaped your wealth on yourself, bought trappings to bolster your worth, and closed your ears to the needy that you experience emotional unrest. Remember the story of John D. Rockefeller discussed in the previous chapter and how his giving extended his life and brought him great peace and satisfaction.

Relationships. God and family—in that order—must occupy their rightful places in our hearts *and* schedules. The media bombards us weekly with the news of the latest breakup between couples who have achieved fame and fortune. Hollywood divorces are now a cliché. Unfortunately, relationship failures are not limited to Hollywood. Divorces are also becoming increasingly prevalent among God's leaders and lay people. Ministers wrongly prioritize ministry over their families—all in the name of serving God. Some have even convinced their wives that it is an acceptable priority with God. The wives resort to frustration and quiet resentment. Even though the minister may achieve public success, he is indeed a private failure in God's eyes.

When couples split, it is evident that one or both parties are out of step with God's mandates for successful relationships. I'll never forget the advice of Mr. Jones, our high school band instructor. As a rhythm-challenged majorette, I couldn't seem to stay on the same foot with the other majorettes when we marched. I tried getting in step with the one to my left, then the one to my right—all to no avail. "Left, right, left, left...oops, off again!" One day during practice, Mr. Jones yelled, "Smith, stop looking to the left or the right. Just keep your eyes on the drum major. Everybody who is in step with the drum major will be in step with each other!" How true. When we fail to make God the drum major in our lives, we march to the beat of the world. Our relationships suffer and peace of mind eludes us.

E—Expect More from God and Less from People

Have you ever had high expectations of someone who failed you or dashed your hopes? Such experiences can cause us to become very insecure in our relationships. If not careful, we start to paint everyone with the same broad behavior brush. What we have to remember is that human beings are prone to disappointing us—not necessarily on purpose but simply because they are mere humans, made from the dust of the earth. We must emulate our Father and extend grace to them. "As a father has compassion on his children, so the LORD has compassion on those who fear him; for he knows how we are formed, he remembers that we are dust" (Psalm 103:13-14). On her dying bed, my mentor the late Dr. Juanita Smith explained how she had dealt with people who had disappointed or hurt her. She said, "We all hurt people. Many times people don't know the extent to which they have hurt us. That's why we have to release everybody. We have to forgive." She knew God had a divine purpose in allowing her to suffer failed expectations; she also knew He had given her grace to endure them.

We cannot afford to get stuck in insecurity or unforgiveness because someone fails to meet our expectations. The best we can do is to pray for the people in our lives to be submissive to God's ways and expect God to answer our prayers on their behalf. If you want to cultivate peace in your life, settle this truth in your heart and learn to redirect your expectations to God. The psalmist cautioned himself, "My soul, wait thou only upon God; for my expectation is from him" (Psalm 62:5 KJV). Whatever anyone does toward us, we must always be mindful that God could have stopped them at any point along the way, but He chose not to. Obviously, He deemed our spiritual growth and maturity a more important necessity.

Even though the all-knowing God is never disappointed, shocked, or surprised by human behavior, He is hurt nevertheless when we violate His laws. Imagine how it saddened Him when He saw His creation become totally corrupt. "The LORD saw how great man's wickedness on the earth had become, and that every inclination of the thoughts of his heart was only evil all the time. The LORD was grieved that he had made man on the earth, and his heart was filled with pain" (Genesis 6:5-6). God decided to destroy everything and start all over again. However, "Noah found favor in the eyes of the LORD" (Genesis 6:8). Because Noah was an upright man, God used him and his family to repopulate the earth after He sent the great flood. No matter how strong the temptation, we must not write off all men or all women or the whole human race just because people seem to continuously fail our expectations. To experience peace, we must believe that God will send the right people, though imperfect, who will fulfill our needs and be worthy of our trust.

A—Acknowledge God in All Your Decisions.

Because most of us tend to act like "human doings" rather than "human beings," we don't invest the necessary time to ascertain whether we are in God's will or not. Rather, we immediately pursue the first great-sounding idea that pops in our minds. Nothing is more frustrating than to find that after you have expended tremendous effort on an endeavor, God comes along and says, "No."

Jehoshaphat, one of the good kings of Judah, was fit to be tied. He had entered into a partnership with the wicked king of Israel to construct a fleet of trading ships. He did what a lot of us do and failed to acknowledge God before he entered the agreement. God is adamant about not being unequally yoked in any situation with an unbeliever. He was not about to set a precedent or reward that kind of independence even for this king, who walked uprightly before him. He sent a prophet to deliver the devastating message to Jehoshaphat: "'Because you have made an alliance with Ahaziah, the LORD will destroy what you have made.' The ships were wrecked and were not able to set sail to trade" (2 Chronicles 20:37). Think of all the capital expenditures, the labor cost, and the mental energy that went into such an undertaking. Nothing was recouped; it had all been done in vain. Such a major failure can deal a powerful blow to one's ego and sense of adequacy.

When we go on independent excursions through life and come to the end of ourselves and realize our mistake, we expect God to help us. Sometimes He extends grace and bails us out; other times He sits back and allows us to learn the lesson that every *good* idea is not a *God* idea. King Solomon warned us against following our own natural instincts. "Trust in the LORD with all your heart; do not depend on your own understanding.

Seek his will in all you do, and he will direct your paths" (Proverbs 3:5-6 NLT).

C—Cultivate an Attitude of Contentment.

Emotionally secure people have *learned* how to practice peace. Learning is not an instant process; it implies studying and applying concepts. The apostle Paul said, "I have learned to be content whatever the circumstances. I know what it is to be in need, and I know what it is to have plenty. I have learned the secret of being content in any and every situation, whether well fed or hungry, whether living in plenty or in want" (Philippians 4:11-12).

> *Prosperity does not have the power to give us contentment, nor poverty the power to take it away.*

When you cultivate an attitude of contentment with every aspect of your life, you are no longer susceptible to the media's or anyone else's assertion that you are "less than" and "need more." No one can convince you that some "thing" is going to bring you fulfillment and satisfaction. "But," you may ask, "suppose I do want more? Am I to be satisfied with living a mediocre life? Are you advocating complacency?" No way.

I'm advocating an attitude of gratitude for what you already have and the faith to believe that God sees your request for more and will grant you what you need and desire at an appointed time. Some people have engaged in either-or thinking and assumed that God wants them to have very little. As such, they extol the virtues of poverty and the denial of material things as the key to peace and contentment. Bible teacher Chip Ingram said on a recent broadcast, "Prosperity does not have the power to give us contentment, nor poverty the power to take it away."

E—Eliminate All Unrighteousness

The prophet Isaiah proclaimed, "The fruit of righteousness will be peace; the effect of righteousness will be quietness and confidence forever" (Isaiah 32:17). Righteousness is simply being in right standing with God. Walking uprightly before Him is foundational to inner peace. We have to make the connection and understand that "righteousness and peace kiss each other" (Psalm 85:10). There is an intimate relationship between doing right and experiencing peace. Sin disconnects us from our power source, the one and only God who enables us to be adequate and sufficient for every task. High moral living puts you under the umbrella of His protection and shields you from the uncertainty that haunts those who are disobedient.

By no means am I implying that to be emotionally secure you must live a sinless life 24 hours a day. Our Father knew we would sin, so He sent Jesus to atone for all of our transgressions. Our responsibility in this process is twofold: first, to quickly repent of every sin so that we can immediately reestablish our connection with a holy God, and second, to invoke the Holy Spirit to keep us from repeat performances of the wrongdoing.

Let's say your insecurity causes you to lie by implying you have a certain level of assets or that you have close relationships with certain "important" people. You know your exaggeration is really a form of lying, but it seems to work for you by getting you the attention and admiration you desire. What do you do? Continue to be dishonest? Of course not. You realize your behavior is jeopardizing your relationship with your heavenly Father, on whom you depend for your daily existence. You make a decision to be authentic, to appreciate whatever talents and gifts you have been given, and to rely on God rather than on lies to give you favor with people.

There is a calm assurance, a noticeable sense of peace that emanates from those whose trust is in the Lord. They do not have a scarcity mentality that causes them to hesitate to help

> *S*ecure people walk in peace because they have learned to put their negative thoughts *to rest* even though their negative circumstances *may prevail.*

others; they joyously cooperate. They know their destiny is sealed. Secure people walk in peace because they have learned to put their negative *thoughts* to rest even though their negative *circumstances* may prevail. They are free of emotional turbulence. They know that to walk in Supreme confidence, they must cast down every thought that is inconsistent with what they know about God. They practice living by faith, rather than by what they feel or see. They have stopped fearing alienation and abandonment. They trust God to guard their relationships.

Experiencing the peace that characterizes the life of emotionally secure people requires a complete surrendering of our will, ambitions, and desires to the One who knows our lives from start to finish. It means staying conscious on a moment by moment basis of the empowering presence of a caring Father.

CONFIDENCE CHALLENGE

&· Having embraced the truth of Psalm 139:16 that reminds us that all of the days ordained for us were written in His book before one of them came to be, name one thing that you have decided to stop fretting about.

&· How will your behavior or conversation change as a result of this decision?

Walking in Victory

SOMETIMES YOU HAVE TO BEHAVE your way to victory. Simply put, you must begin to act like an emotionally secure person. Now that you have sought the Lord and accepted by faith that He has delivered you from your fears, you can begin to genuinely model the behavior of a secure person. Emotions follow behavior. You will begin to feel more secure when you start to engage in secure behavior.

As David ran toward the physically intimidating Philistine giant, so must we learn to run toward the emotionally intimidating giant of insecurity. We must not take an ostrichlike approach and pretend that insecurity is not there; we cannot be healed from that which we have concealed. We must confess our insecurity and conquer it with the Word of God.

Amassing worldly trappings, such as designer clothes, fancy cars, loads of money, or a list of influential friends, will be as ineffective in curing insecurity as a putting a Band-Aid on cancer. Facades of confidence are just that—facades; they will not defeat insecurity. We must slay this giant with spiritual weapons.

The principles of overcoming insecurity are as simple as ABCD:

- A—Acknowledge your core fear. Self-deception will keep you in the pit of insecurity.
- B—Believe that God can and will deliver you. Nothing is too hard for Him.
- C—Change your thoughts. Behavior follows belief. Cast down every thought of inadequacy and all other security-robbing imaginations.
- D—Decree your victory from the Word of God. His Word will heal all of your ills.

These steps are simple but not easy. You must become like the remora fish and stay connected to an omnipotent, omniscient, and omnipresent God. Daily confess:

"I am surrounded with the favor of God. I am safe, sure, sufficient. I am secure."

South African president Nelson Mandela, in his 1994 inaugural address, eloquently stated,

> Our deepest fear is not that we are inadequate. Our deepest fear is that we are powerful beyond measure. It is our light, not our darkness that frightens us. We ask ourselves, who am I to be brilliant, gorgeous, talented, and fabulous? Actually, who are we not to be? You are a child of God. Your playing small doesn't serve the world. There's nothing enlightened about shrinking so that other people won't feel insecure around you. We were born to make manifest the glory of God that is within us. It's not just in some of us; it's in everyone. And as we let our own light shine, we unconsciously give other people permission to do the same. As we are liberated from our own fears, our presence automatically liberates others.

Healing Prayer for Insecurity

ATHER, I COME BOLDLY before Your throne of grace to obtain mercy and find grace for deliverance from emotional insecurity (Hebrews 4:16 NKJV).

I stand on Your Word that assures me that You are able to make all of Your grace abound toward me so that I will always have all sufficiency in all things and will abound in every good work (2 Corinthians 9:8).

I cast down every thought of inadequacy and every imagination that rises up against what Your Word says about who I am and what I can do (2 Corinthians 10:5 KJV).

I resist any anxiety over the possibility of losing a social, professional, or other position, or a desired relationship. I know that no one can thwart Your purpose for my life. You, O Lord, have sealed my destiny (Isaiah 14:27) and You guard all that is mine (Psalm 16:5 NLT).

Thank You, Father, for my unchangeable physical features (height, race, hair, complexion, etc.). I repent for all of the times

I rejected Your design and allowed insecurity to creep in because of worldly standards. I know, according to Your Word, that You deliberately shaped me in the womb to be Your servant. Therefore, I rest and rejoice in the truth that I am designed for my destiny and am perfect for my purpose (Isaiah 49:5).

Because of Your grace, I walk neither in self-doubt nor in self-confidence because I know that apart from You I can do absolutely nothing (John 15:5). Therefore, my eyes are on You alone to do exceedingly, abundantly above all that I could ask or think according to your Power that works in me (Ephesians 3:20 NKJV).

I thank You that as I have prayed, You have heard me and delivered me from all my fears; they no longer have any power over my life (Psalm 34:4 NKJV).

Thank You for the Supreme confidence that is mine because I am connected to You, my all-powerful, all-knowing, and always-present Father. In the name of Jesus Christ, I pray. Amen.

Insecurity-Banishing Scriptures

A<small>S CHILDREN OF</small> G<small>OD</small> in a battle to overcome insecurity and to walk in Supreme confidence, we must keep an arsenal of Scriptures hidden in our hearts so that we may quickly respond to the attacks of Satan. He only respects the Word of God. We must be able to confidently say, "It is written…" If we do not know what is written, we will not know that a thought has risen up against what God has said about who we are and what we can do. Negative thoughts must be cast down with a word from the Word. Below is a sampling of Scriptures to hide in your heart as defensive and offensive weapons for conquering insecurity.

Those who fear the L<small>ORD</small> are secure (Proverbs 14:26 <small>NLT</small>).

I am the vine; you are the branches. If a man remains in me and I in him, he will bear much fruit; apart from me you can do nothing (John 15:5).

Not that we are adequate in ourselves to consider anything as coming from ourselves, but our adequacy is from God (2 Corinthians 3:5 NASB).

We are more than conquerors through him that loved us (Romans 8:37 KJV).

His divine power has given us everything we need for life and godliness through our knowledge of him who called us by his own glory and goodness (2 Peter 1:3).

This is the confidence we have in approaching God: that if we ask anything according to his will, he hears us. And if we know that he hears us—whatever we ask—we know that we have what we asked of him (1 John 5:14-15).

For the eyes of the LORD range throughout the earth to strengthen those whose hearts are fully committed to him (2 Chronicles 16:9).

I sought the LORD, and He heard me, and delivered me from all my fears (Psalm 34:4 NKJV).

Be anxious for nothing, but in everything by prayer and supplication, with thanksgiving, let your requests be made known to God; and the peace of God, which surpasses all understanding, will guard your hearts and minds through Christ Jesus (Philippians 4:6-7 NKJV).

And God is able to make all grace abound to you, so that in all things at all times, having all that you need, you will abound in every good work (2 Corinthians 9:8).

"No weapon forged against you will prevail, and you will refute every tongue that accuses you. This is the heritage of the servants of the LORD, and this is their vindication from me," declares the LORD (Isaiah 54:17).

And we know that all things work together for good to those who love God, to those who are the called according to His purpose (Romans 8:28 NKJV).

For the LORD shall be thy confidence (Proverbs 3:26 KJV).

When I am afraid, I will trust in you (Psalm 56:3).

For God did not give us a spirit of timidity, but a spirit of power, of love and of self-discipline (2 Timothy 1:7).

Dear friends, if our conscience is clear, we can come to God with bold confidence. And we will receive whatever we request because we obey him and do the things that please him (1 John 3:21-22 NLT).

The fruit of righteousness will be peace; the effect of righteousness will be quietness and confidence forever (Isaiah 32:17).

For surely, O LORD, you bless the righteous; you surround them with your favor as with a shield (Psalm 5:12).

For you have been my hope, O Sovereign LORD, my confidence since my youth. From birth I have relied on you (Psalm 71:5-6).

Blessed is the man who trusts in the LORD, whose confidence is in him. He will be like a tree planted by the water that sends out its roots by the stream. It does not fear when heat comes; its leaves are always green. It has no worries in a year of drought and never fails to bear fruit (Jeremiah 17:7-8).

Let us then approach the throne of grace with confidence, so that we may receive mercy and find grace to help us in our time of need (Hebrews 4:16).

So we say with confidence, "The Lord is my helper; I will not be afraid. What can man do to me?" (Hebrews 13:6).

He who trusts in himself is a fool, but he who walks in wisdom is kept safe (Proverbs 28:26).

You saw me before I was born and scheduled each day of my life before I began to breathe. Every day was recorded in your book! (Psalm 139:16 TLB).

Being confident of this, that he who began a good work in you will carry it on to completion until the day of Christ Jesus (Philippians 1:6).

Be sure of this—that I am with you always, even to the end of the world (Matthew 28:20 TLB).

The name of the LORD is a strong tower; the righteous run to it and are safe (Proverbs 18:10).

Endnotes

1. Paul Lee Tan, *Encyclopedia of 7700 Illustrations*, Garland, TX: Bible Communications, 1996, #2671.
2. David Viscott, *Emotionally Free* (Chicago, IL: Contemporary Books, 1992) p. 54.
3. <nh.essortment.com/rogerbannister_rzqk.htm>.
4. <outside.away.com/magazine/1099/199910hillary1.html>.
5. "On the Way to the Top," *Bits & Pieces,* December 2004, p. 9.
6. <outside.away.com/magazine/1099/199910hillary1.html>.
7. Deborah Smith Pegues, *Show Me the Money!* (Los Angeles, CA: Wisdom Publishing, 2000), pp. 106-07.

How to Contact the Author

*D*eborah Smith Pegues is an experienced certified public accountant, a Bible teacher, a speaker, a certified behavioral consultant specializing in understanding personality temperaments, and the author of *30 Days to Taming Your Tongue*. She and her husband, Darnell, have been married for more than 25 years and make their home in California.

For speaking engagements, please contact the author at:

The Pegues Group
P.O. Box 56382
Los Angeles, California 90056
(323) 293-5861

or

E-mail: ddpegues@sbcglobal.net
www.confrontingissues.com

*A*lso by Deborah Smith Pegues at www.confrontingissues.com:

Managing Conflict God's Way: Biblical Strategies for Effective Confrontations

"Show Me the Money!": Uncovering the Eight Pitfalls to Financial Freedom